The Window Box
POT, TUB & BASKET BOOK

The Window Box
POT, TUB & BASKET BOOK

DIANA STEWART
ILLUSTRATED BY MARILYN LEADER

You can do your bit for conservation by planting unusual wild flower seeds. If chosen for the local soil they may seed and re-establish themselves in the district. Children can be involved in a project of this kind, which can be quite inexpensive yet attractive if containers are improvised from old oil drums or dustbins and painted in pretty colours.

HEARST BOOKS

Text Copyright © 1985 by Diana Stewart
Illustrations Copyright © 1985 by Breslich & Foss

Designed and produced by
Breslich & Foss, London

Full-colour plates by Marilyn Leader
Two-colour drawings by Lorna Turpin

Library of Congress Catalog Card Number: 84-62388

ISBN: 0−688−03984−7

Printed in Spain
First U.S. Edition
1 2 3 4 5 6 7 8 9 10

CONTENTS

FOREWORD

Box, pot or planter, *jardinière*, *balconnière* or urn, it seems there is no end to the names for containers, attractive and not so attractive, that can be used for growing flowers and plants.

In the end I settled for box. A nice, simple, short word, Old English in origin and with a happy connection with the evergreen plant of that name much regarded by early workers in wood. They may well have used it for early window boxes.

Certainly there is nothing new about the practice of growing plants in boxes rather than in the open ground. The Middle East is said to have been the cradle of civilization and in the Middle East water is a valued commodity. When you have hauled water from a well—and been glad to find it there at all— you do not willingly pour it back into the ground. Since plants must be watered, it makes better sense to contain the plants and conserve the water.

Containerization, the method by which plants are kept in marketable condition throughout the year, is relatively new, although there must be a generation of gardeners now who have never had to order roses in the summer for delivery, with bare roots, from November onwards. Containerized plants gave us the garden centre, open on Sundays when we most need it. And if we go a bit mad on Sunday morning and don't manage to get all our purchases into the ground that day, well, there is no harm done. They can stay in their containers until next weekend when we have more time.

From here it is only a short step to keeping them in a container permanently. 'I've nowhere to put it,' is my first anguished thought when I spot some treasure I have long coveted. It may not be there next time I call and if it is then it will still be in its same container. So buy it now and transfer it from

its black plastic bag to a more attractive box or pot, planter or *jardinière*. Whether this is a wooden or plastic box on a window sill or a large clay pot, an elegant white-painted wheeled contraption or a roughly painted oil drum is immaterial. If the pot in which a plant is sold can be comfortably accommodated in another container then all is well. For a while, at least. An oak tree will probably survive in a 10 inch clay pot for a few years but eventually its roots will break it. Even before this happens it may well not be a very happy oak tree. But if it is your fancy to have an oak tree on your patio then you may have one, even if only temporarily.

A box is often no more than a temporary home, but the planning and planting of it can be a permanent source of satisfaction.

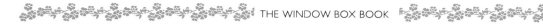
First Steps

SITING AND INSTALLATION

It may not at first seem difficult to decide where to site a window box: you put it on the window ledge, of course—until you realize that your windows have no ledges, or only narrow ones, or that you won't be able to open a casement window without damaging the taller plants. You may even realize that once plants really get going they will shut out the light, plunging your rooms into jungle-like gloom just when they might have been filled with sun.

Ingenious answers may come to mind—mounting a box on a shelf below the sills, for instance, so as not to keep light out. But before dealing with problems piecemeal it is better to stand back and see whether they can be tackled another way.

Think first why you want window boxes at all. After all, they will need a lot of upkeep if they are to stay looking good. Window boxes are most commonly used to brighten up a house fascia, to make the house stand out from its near-identical neighbours. The gentrification of down-at-heel streets often begins with a few tentative window boxes alongside the dolphin door knockers and carriage lamps. Then, in no time at all it seems, the

Before you know it the whole street is ablaze with window boxes.

8

whole street is ablaze with summer geraniums and you find you are now living in what real estate agents are pleased to call a much-sought-after area, with price tags to match. Whether or not you approve of this, it is a fact that one window box does lead to another, as neighbours see what instant transformation they can impose on an otherwise unremarkable property.

These bright, attractive boxes are usually installed

The flat two-dimensional appearance will be exaggerated in a sketch or snap, showing clearly where boxes can effect a transformation.

by people whose interest in gardening is minimal; they are there for decorative effect only and are thus usually put at the front of the house where they can be most admired.

Other window box gardeners are motivated by the need to have a garden to cultivate and soil to get their hands into, even if minimal in quantity. They have already filled every conceivable indoor ledge with plants and will now be bursting outwards with an urge that may never be requited until they have exchanged their city apartment for a rural retreat and four acres and a cow. The window boxes of these frustrated city gardeners are not restricted to the front of the house but can be seen clinging to every get-at-able spot, front, back and sides. Front boxes will be planned for effect but boxes at the back may be less decorative—from the outside at least—and may be designed for viewing from inside, or to satisfy a desire for fresh herbs, fresh salads, vegetables, tomatoes, cucumbers. They may house a collection of alpines, or provide summer quarters for a cactus collection.

So before rushing out and buying a window box it is worth spending a few moments examining your objectives. If you are aiming for decorative effect it is not a bad idea to take a photograph or make a

rough sketch of the front of the house. On this, or on tracing paper taped over the picture, you can sketch in boxes at various windows and assess the effect. The flat, two-dimensional appearance will be exaggerated in a quick sketch or photo and may show you more clearly where window boxes can effect a transformation. A deep window ledge may seem the obvious place for a box that can be bought or constructed to nearly fill the length leaving, if access is possible from inside the house only, just enough space for you to lift the box and bring it inside. But this concentration of colour may serve only to emphasize a narrow window, or a tall narrow house. Sketch in a wider box, standing on a stout shelf fixed with brackets just below the sill, and you may see how this widens the window visually. You can also use window boxes to tidy up the effect of odd-sized windows, a common problem in some older houses.

Studying the lines of the house carefully may show you that there are a number of better sites for your window box than the obvious window sill. At ground level beneath the windows, for instance, if your house is surrounded by a concrete apron that is supposed to make it easier to clean the windows but that actually only prevents you growing plants up

Window boxes can tidy up the effect of odd-sized windows.

the walls. A window box will change all that; you can have roses, vines, honeysuckle, even ivy, planted in a ground-level window box.

If your front door has a projecting porch that is stout enough to take the weight, this can be an excellent site for a box, enabling you to grow both

trailers and climbers to frame the door. You will need to be able to reach it for watering, of course, and should exercise a certain amount of caution when choosing plants so as not to obstruct the door.

The flat roof of a garage can be another useful site. Don't get carried away and start thinking about roof gardens. These are another thing altogether, for they involve enormous weight and often structural alterations. But a box that extends across the front of the garage can cheer up its looks no end. Here plants should not trail; it is difficult enough getting into the average garage without having to drive around trails of herbage.

Then there are those ugly projections that so often occur in houses that have undergone multiple conversions. Builders seal off some feature no longer needed, slap cement all around and the result is hideous, but if it is used as a home for window boxes it immediately recedes from view. An easily moved box is often the suggestion for concealing an ugly manhole, and it is true that this is an answer as long as the box itself does not stick out at the same awkward angle. Builders have an unerring talent for putting their manholes just where they cannot be concealed. This is probably the object of the exercise, but in thirty years of trying to conceal

manhole covers with easily moved boxes I have never actually been required to move one. So if you can make use of such a spot, do so.

Railings or the parapet of a balcony can be an excellent spot from which to hang window boxes. For safety and ease of maintenance, hang them inside the balcony. For maximum light, let the box hang over the outer edge of the railing or balcony. If there is a roof above that cuts out light, you will find that flowers grow at an angle to reach both the light and any rain that is going. This can make the effect from the balcony side rather disappointing—like seeing a magnificent herbaceous border from its stalky back. If you put trailers at the outside these will arch nicely to reach the light, then you can position short and shade-loving plants at the front for your own benefit.

Apartment dwellers, especially those who live in tall buildings, will know only too well the wind-tunnel effect of these. This increases the higher up the building you go, with consequent effect on plant life. The answer is to plant firmly, to stake plants if they are at all fragile or protect them with chicken wire, and to choose only low-growing varieties. Trailers can be encouraged to trail back out of the wind—they will be only too glad to do so

anyway—and can be cut at the growing tips to make short clumpy trails rather than long straggly ones.

Wind can do more than disturb plants—a freak gust can actually lift a whole box—so before installing a box anywhere where it could conceivably fall and hurt persons or property below, make sure that it is securely positioned. Don't rely on the weight of the box alone to hold it firm; use brackets to keep it in place.

Check the condition of window and other ledges, or get a builder to do so. Check the state of your household insurance too—are you sufficiently covered if a falling flower-pot hits the milkman on the head, or will you be paying him, his dependants and his lawyers a lifelong pension? Today third party insurance is usually included in household insurance, but it is as well to make sure. You may also need to check your lease, or get your landlord's or local authority's permission before putting up window boxes and this may come with its own provisos on safety. Still on the subject of safety, never keep loose pots or your window box tools on the window sills. These can so easily be dislodged and, falling at speed, inflict awful damage.

Your own personal safety is another big consideration. Keeping a box well watered should

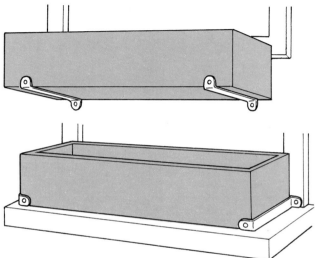

Use brackets to hold a box in place, either below or at window sill level.

not entail wobbling about on a rickety chair to reach it. You should also seek help in lifting a heavy box into position if you don't want your gardening career cut off in its prime. Keep a firm step-ladder where you, and not burglars, can easily reach it and use it whenever necessary. Safety aside, it is much more pleasant, and much less of a chore, to do all the jobs like watering and forking over and nipping out and tidying up from a comfortable position rather than from an unsafe one.

WATERING AND MAINTENANCE

As I shall probably repeat *ad nauseam*, window boxes need regular watering. This means, in very hot weather and/or in a very sunny position, as often as twice or even three times a day. It is not only hot sun that dries out a window box; that combination of bright sun and crisp wind that sometimes bedevils summers can be equally hard on plant life because it dries out both compost and containers.

Regular watering, even if it does mean postponing for a few minutes your homecoming cup of coffee or glass of wine, actually saves you time. The compost in a box can dry out six ways: through the open-to-the-air surface at the top, obviously, then through all four sides and through the bottom. Compare this to the soil in the garden, which can only dry out one way—upwards—and you will see why window boxes need so much watering. Even when there is no sun the warmer, drier atmosphere around the box constantly draws out moisture. The same applies to the winter when roots, instead of being nicely tucked away underground, are exposed on all sides to extreme temperatures. In hot

weather, as the soil in a box dries, it shrinks away from the sides. Since water will always take the easiest route to the water table, the contents of the next watering can will run straight down the sides of the box instead of seeping gently through the compost to the root balls of the plants. These will become progressively drier, and usually the only way to get water to the roots of dried-out plants is to immerse the container completely for half an hour or so, until all the air has bubbled out and the water has really permeated the compost. This can be a job and a half if the box is a large one, so you can see that it does save time to water regularly.

Before you site your box think how water can most easily be taken to it. This might be with a convenient length of hose coming from a kitchen, bathroom or outside tap. If so, cut your hose to size, add a connector, and find a convenient place to store it at the same time as you do up the box. Then watering will be a simple matter right from the start and this, I promise you, will be reflected in the vigour of the plants.

If you have nothing so convenient as water on tap,

you will have to rely on cans. If you can keep these, ready filled, close to the box all the better. One can per box is not a bad idea if it saves you carting water from the other side of the house, or from one room to another. The cans, either plastic or galvanized, can look quite decorative provided they are kept clean. Galvanized cans don't seem to suffer from algae; plastic ones, which do, can be kept clean by regular washing out with an algicide. One tiny city patio I used to pass regularly had two matching galvanized cans painted fire engine red and elegantly arranged among the boxes and tubs. One held water and the other had itself been planted with seasonal flowers. If you have to buy a can specially, have a look at some of the pressure sprayers that are available in various sizes. These cost a bit more but, as they come with long hoses and long-reach nozzles, allow water to be applied without your having to lift the can off the ground. A boon if you have a bad back, or don't want to acquire one. You simply pump up pressure then adjust the nozzle to emit anything from a fine mist to a jet of water. The jet can be directed close to plant roots, so the water is not slopped messily and wastefully over the sides of the box. You can then switch to the fine spray and give the leaves the all-over misting that they love. A

gardener, accustomed to using a pressure sprayer to apply insecticides in quantity to roses or fruit trees, might laugh at the idea of a mere window box gardener employing one, but I promise you that this can be a very useful tool.

Even if you can't provide, or haven't room for, a watering can or sprayer, you should try to hide a container full of water somewhere nearby. I find that keeping a large plastic squash container right beside them is the only way I can ensure two of my hanging baskets are properly watered. I really shouldn't have put them in such an out-of-the-way and hard-to-water spot, but I wanted the splash of colour they made in the summer. Having the water at hand means that I do the job then and there and the plants don't suffer. The containers are brought inside afterwards for refilling, which can be done 'when I have a minute'.

If watering must be done from inside the house, you will need an old sheet or mat to spread over carpets or parquet. Keep it handy and you will use it; put it away neatly in another room and you will be tempted to manage without it one day and that's when the damage will be done.

Regular watering is even more important if you have to work from indoors, because even a

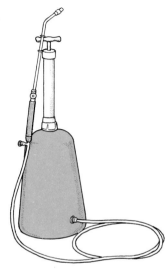

Pressure sprayers are available in various sizes and allow water to be applied without lifting.

lightweight plastic can weighs an immense amount when filled. If it has to be held at waist level or higher while you give a dried-out box a really good soak this can be very tiring. Better to water little and often or treat yourself to a pressure sprayer. The 'little and often' treatment can be death to indoor plants, of course, but this is unlikely to be the case with a window box. Only if a box is completely without drainage holes and is then regularly and unfailingly watered is it likely to become overwatered. The importance of adequate drainage from window boxes is, to my mind, often overstressed. I certainly have rarely known a waterlogged box and most of the time the problem is to keep the compost from drying out.

Nevertheless every box must have holes in the bottom or the lower layers will collect sour water. Purpose-made wooden or stone boxes are usually sold with holes ready drilled; plastic ones generally come with indentations that you can tap out with a small screwdriver to make as many or as few holes as you choose. I would always make the maximum number and then fit a drip-tray. These really are essential. If drips run down walls they make dirty, and then mossy marks. If they spill out over the edge they can make a mess of the downstairs windows, or even of the people downstairs. The box should not lie directly on the tray but be supported on small feet so that there is air beneath it. If you notice that the tray is constantly full of water you can deduce that you are watering a bit too enthusiastically. If you notice instead that the water that drips through at first has almost dried out by the next watering you will know that you are creating that slightly damp micro-climate in which plants flourish.

Knowing just how much water to give, especially when a box is newly planted and roots have not had time to make much growth, is what separates the expert gardener from the novice. Plants in window boxes, with their restricted root run, respond to underwatering by flopping very quickly. This should not be allowed to happen because it gives them a setback from which they never properly recover. A plant that is not giving of its best can be tolerated perhaps in the open garden where there is plenty else going on, but in a window box all the occupants must be successes or the decorative effect is lost.

Overwatering is scarcely possible in high summer when plants have grown fully and root balls have extended to fill the box. Before this, yes, you can overwater. Waterlogged soil looks flat and sour and soon starts to grow moss; if you think you have been

overdoing things, stir up the top layer of soil to let the air in, scrape off any moss or liverworts and ease up on the watering until the compost seems drier. Plant roots need air as well as water and expelling all the air from the compost and replacing it with water causes the roots to rot away. If you take life very seriously you could buy a moisture meter and check whether your watering is right or not. But it is better to learn the feel of well-watered soil, using the fingers you were born with; it doesn't take very long.

Capillary benching has all but transformed the lives of commercial growers, offering a foolproof method of keeping growing plants regularly supplied with water without incurring enormous labour costs. There is nothing new about the idea of letting moisture seep from one medium to another—damp sand for instance to the compost in a pot. The same principle applies when you rig up a holiday watering system for your indoor plants, standing them on damp newspaper in the bath and leaving a tap dripping, or running individual wicks from a central reservoir—a bucket filled with water—to each plant pot. Either way the compost, as long as it is damp to start with, will stay damp as long as the newspaper or wick remains in contact with water

and doesn't itself become dry.

Capillary matting and wicks can be expensive, especially if you need a lot of them, and it might pay to experiment with strips of old sheeting or even old long bootlaces if these can be concealed while still being effective. Sink a container into the compost in the box when you first put in the plants, then keep it filled and run your wicks, laces or whatever along to each plant. If you do this in advance of your holiday, you can check how effective it is before you go away and how long the reservoir can be expected to last before drying up. Remember that in very hot weather there can be considerable evaporation. Window boxes are demanding dependants and when the summer comes and beach, tennis courts and the great outdoors beckon it is only too easy to 'forget' the twice daily watering programme. The soil gets drier and drier and what water you give becomes less effective, running down the sides of the box and bypassing the roots entirely. Result: one very unhappy window box whose occupants have received so severe a setback that they will never really give of their best. Far better to admit that you are less than perfect and rig up a system that keeps the box happy and lets you off the hook for longer.

CHOOSING A BOX

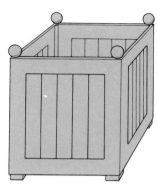

A Versailles Pot, often used for a bay tree in a town garden.

When you have decided where you are going to install your window boxes and are ready to choose them you may be less than enthusiastic about the ones you see for sale in garden centres or in the garden sections of supermarkets. Plastic predominates, often in a curiously unnatural shade of green, and the alternatives, of reconstituted stone or terracotta, range from the beautiful but wickedly expensive to the downright cheap and nasty. Wood is still used for tubs, the half-barrel type with metal hoops that have a rustic cottagey look that is nice in the right place. It can also be used for what are known as Versailles pots, elegant square boxes, usually painted white and often provided with wheels for easy moving. These are reproductions of those used in eighteenth century orangeries, the wheels allowing the orange and lemon trees to be moved out into the sun for summer; they look splendid housing twin bay trees beside a Georgian front door and are usually priced to match.

Simple plain wooden boxes seem rather thin on the ground, it being usually assumed that these can be put together more cheaply by the average handyman. When you come to investigate the boxes you pass on your travels the chances are that many of those you like best are, in fact, purpose-built in wood. If you can make boxes yourself, or find someone to make them for you, you will have the advantage of ones that fit the window sills for which they are intended. The combined cost of wood and wood preservative and/or paint will probably come to more than you expected but remember that, given routine maintenance, wooden boxes can be expected to last a good few years. Before making a start on your own boxes, however, you should bear in mind certain inescapable precepts.

1 The smaller the box, the faster it will dry out, the more it will need watering and the less impact it will have.
2 The larger the box, the heavier it will be, the more difficult to manoeuvre into position or to remove for replanting, the more important it is to make it secure and the more impact it will have.

Before embarking on the construction of a very small box to fit a very small window, remember

precept number 1. On an 18 inch window sill I might just install a standard size plastic box 17 × 5 × 4½ inches deep. This would allow for the comfortable planting of three plants bought in 3½ inch pots, the usual size in which summer bedders like geraniums or spring subjects such as polyanthus are sold. The impact of just three plants would not, it must be admitted, be very dramatic seen from a distance. On the other hand, you often find just such a window alongside the front door and here the box would be seen and enjoyed by everyone coming to the house. Watering would be no problem either; every time you put out a milk bottle you would fill it first with clean water and simply empty it into the box.

Wooden boxes can be fashioned, rustic style, in hardwood such as cedar if you can get hold of it. This will need treatment, inside and out, every couple of years with one of the wood preservatives designed especially for greenhouse use. These shouldn't harm plants, but check the instructions carefully before using them. They come in a terracotta shade that enriches faded red cedar and that also looks attractive painted onto plain deal or pine. There is also a rather livid green for use on greenhouse staging that I personally dislike until it has faded so much it really needs renewing. Green is

a very difficult colour to put with growing things. When you look hard at a leaf, or a stretch of lawn, you can see that it is actually made up of a dozen or more greens, often with as many greys or yellows or reds. One single shade of green, no matter how attractive in its own right, looks unnatural against this rich variety of shades; brown, black, terracotta or white are usually a safer choice.

More formal boxes invariably benefit from being painted white, especially if the surrounding house paintwork is also white. The only disadvantage is that this means regular repainting, because dirty marks and moss soon build up. Stone or terracotta improves with weathering—although moss should be scrubbed off occasionally—but paint should always be fresh. Coloured paintwork is a temptation that you should try to avoid. If your house has sweetheart shutters in pastel pink you might think that matching window boxes would be a nice touch, until you wanted to plant scarlet geraniums or bright yellow pansies or polyanthus. Bear it in mind.

Stone containers are usually much too heavy for use on window sills and are most frequently used underneath windows at ground level and of course on patios. Stone today is most often a reconstructed version made by pulverizing real stone and binding

Decorated terracotta pot, an ornament in its own right.

it together again, usually in moulds that are cast from genuine antique containers such as water cisterns. The result is remarkably authentic, especially once the weathering and ageing process begins. Prices can be very high. A Venetian trough, say, with fluted supports is not something to dot around the house at will—even one would be a major purchase not to be undertaken lightly—but it certainly would add a touch of class, especially if your house already has class. Slightly less expensive would be a Regency urn, with or without pedestal, or a plaited basket. If you decide to invest in something like this—and I certainly think they are a good investment—take

time over your choice. It would not be too fanciful to suggest making a rough life-size mock-up of the proposed pot or urn from a cardboard box. Stand it in position and study it from all angles. Seen from the front gate a small urn can be completely dwarfed by its surroundings—everything looks smaller out of doors—so that the effect of an expensive purchase could be quite lost. The alternative could only be to spend even more and get a larger urn, or settle for a larger one in a less expensive material.

Terracotta is a good, straightforward material and, used for flower-pots, has stood the test of thousands of years. Handthrown pots are not cheap, but less expensive than stone. A large, straight-sided pot 15 inches in diameter and 12 inches tall, suitable for a massed display of flowers or even a small tree and with an attractive fluted decoration, can be obtained at a very reasonable price. Plain handthrown pots are even cheaper. Decoration always adds to the cost and can be enjoyed while flower growth is low, or during the winter before bulbs appear; but remember that all those decorative swags and rings are often completely hidden in summer by leaves and flowers.

Machine-made terracotta pots are much less

expensive. No, they are not quite as nice as the handthrown variety but, yes, they are an acceptable alternative. Ranged along a house wall or grouped beside a porch or on a patio they blend well with a brick façade. As they are less expensive you can perhaps afford to be bold and to make a splash with a group of descending sized pots rather than just one. When planning a grouping for a small space, on a patio perhaps, another cardboard box mock-up might be an idea. If it seems to clutter the place up or get in the way when you are enjoying a well-earned rest in the sun then it will only get worse once plants start to grow and overhang the sides of the pots.

Stone and terracotta are heavy materials and usually unsuitable for a raised position. Here plastic comes into its own. Now it is fashionable to decry plastic, to equate it with all that is meretricious, and certainly some very unpleasant things are perpetrated today in polypropylene. There are also some very pleasant simple designs that are not to be despised and in fact to be applauded. One in particular has a deep drip-tray that makes watering less of a chore and very slabby modern lines; it comes in either dark brown or beige. There are also self-watering planters with sleek Italian lines.

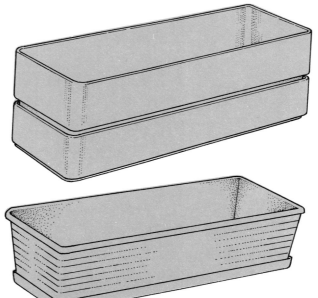

Slabby modern lines plus a deep tray for watering.

A deep drip tray makes watering less of a chore.

At the other end of the scale are those deeply scalloped urns that will never in a month of Sundays resemble the classic designs on which they are loosely based. I wouldn't give them house room. Nor would I a *balconnière* said to be cleverly simulated to look like natural stone that has weathered, to quote its gushing advertising.

Fortunately for all such misconceptions, however, they can often be disguised by lush greenery.

Regard plastic with caution, certainly, but its inescapable advantages are that it is inexpensive and light in weight. Once a box is filled with compost, and once this has been well watered and the flowers have reached full growth, then it can be very heavy indeed. A plastic box and tray $17 \times 5\frac{1}{2} \times 4\frac{1}{2}$ inches, filled with six hyacinths in full flower, weighs, when newly watered, over 10 pounds. As this is the smallest possible size of box—I have one beside the front door and another three in various stages of growth that are interchanged throughout the seasons to give constant colour—you can see that even a box say 5 feet × 7 inches × 6 inches could easily weigh 70 pounds. You can understand what could be involved if you had to move this about very often.

Maintaining a year-round display of colour, variegated leaves in winter followed by spring bulbs and summer bedding plants, is the ideal of many window box gardeners. This can be achieved if you double or treble up your boxes and have some out-of-the-way spot where you can bring the next one on for installation as the first comes to an end. Plastic, the cheapest you can find, would be in order,

and if this turned out also to be the ugliest, you could install a false front across the window sill and drop each plastic box inside as it came into season. The false front can be of painted wood, black or white, or of hardwood treated with preservative; fixing by means of brackets against the wall. When your spring bulbs die down the box can be removed and the summer box installed. It is sometimes difficult to time the first summer flowers to bloom early, especially if you have chosen tender subjects and there is still the danger of frost. In this case a third winter box can be popped into place until the time is right. This means that your windows always look spruce; remember that nothing looks more depressing in early summer than the dying leaves and flowers of spring. You can choose the cheapest material for these inner boxes but beware of too flexible plastic as this can bulge when filled. There are also containers made from something like papier mâché, but I have noticed that these sometimes develop bulges and cracks as root growth increases. Plants are incredibly strong and persistent—think how a weed can actually push its way up through cement or tarmac—and the root ball of many plants can be a sizeable mass of very determined roots.

OTHER CONTAINERS

If you are put off by the price of good containers you can often improvise. Old coal scuttles, saucepans, kettles, catering-size tins, oil drums, even old tyres, can all be filled with soil and given drainage.

Digging over a newly acquired, overgrown garden often turns up discarded galvanized buckets or watering cans; these are too battered to use but can still be filled with plants. Or you might see something appealing in a junk shop or house sale. Builders' merchants often sell old chimney pots and sometimes you can acquire a treasure simply by knocking on a door and asking to buy it. If something is lying on its side in a local garden, the owner may have plans for it or he may be delighted for you to cart it away for him. All it needs is nerve.

Wooden tubs and half barrels are sold by shops and garden centres but can sometimes be picked up more cheaply from factories that have bulk deliveries of raw materials in barrels. Wood containers should be treated inside with one of the proprietary preservatives; don't use creosote or your plants will surely die. Outsides can be painted white and metal parts black, and this paintwork should be freshened up every season. It is a curious feature of container gardening that new containers

Improvise containers from old coal scuttles, kettles or watering cans.

22

An old chimney pot echoes the angular lines of a Victorian house.

look better when they have weathered but improvised ones need to be kept spick and span.

If you can get hold of catering-size tins that have held beans or coffee or oil you can drill holes in the bottoms and paint the outsides and down inside the rims with white paint. An undercoat of metallic paint will help the top coat adhere and will help prolong the useful, if limited, life of this kind of container.

Tyres can often be picked up for nothing and these can be painted white and used singly or in piles of two or three. A combination of different size tyres or a half tyre used as the top layer makes for unusual shapes. But even if you can tap a good source of old tyres, don't get too carried away with the idea; one or two look fine but a whole row looks like a petrol station.

Whenever you use a bottomless container such as a chimney pot or a tyre you should stand it on fine galvanized mesh or even on several layers of old nylon net curtain. This will keep the soil in and woodlice and ants out; ants particularly can burrow away at the soil until plants collapse from lack of support.

All large, and therefore heavy, containers should be set in position before being filled. There is no need to fill them completely with expensive

compost; the lower layers can be built up with broken brick and stones to a more economical depth. This will provide drainage and also stability, an important point if your container is to stand anywhere vulnerable to clumsy visitors or careless milkmen. It is also essential in even the smallest box or container.

Between compost and brick put a layer composed of upturned turf or coarse peat; this will prevent compost washing through.

Suiting container to style of house is very important when the container is an improvised one. Old cottages, particularly when painted white, acquire Gallic charm from olive oil tins filled with cascading geraniums, but their effect on a modern semi could be more ramshackle. Smartly kept houses need smart containers, painted barrels and tubs at the very least. But you can give a modest semi a cottagey look by filling a group of old coal scuttles or a large watering can with plants and setting this beside the front door. An old tall chimney or a group of two or three suits the narrow lines of Victorian villas. Sets of bedroom china, even if badly cracked, can also add to the Victorian air and I have even seen an old loo planted with dandelions, but this is a joke that soon wears thin. The important

thing when choosing any container, especially an unconventional one, is to think big; the great outdoors makes everything look smaller.

Boxes for window sills must, by definition, be long and thin, while expediency might dictate that they should not be too deep. However, anything shallower than 5 or 6 inches or narrower than 6 or 7 inches is liable to prove difficult to keep watered. You might also encounter problems when transferring plants from their usual $3\frac{1}{2}$ inch pots. You should be able to make a neat hole in the damp compost using an empty pot of the same size. Then you can slip a new plant out of its pot and drop it into a matching-sized hole with the minimum of disturbance. Disturbing the roots by squashing them into place seems not to harm some plants, but can set them back and delay flowering. If you are having boxes made then bear this optimum depth in mind; you could reduce the width a little if you had to but you should not reduce the depth.

When the problem is one of almost too much depth, by all means fill the unwanted depth with broken bricks or stones and only the top layers with expensive compost, but if you have the opportunity to offer a slightly deeper root run then do make the most of it, as the plants will undoubtedly benefit.

FILLING

You have selected your box, or boxes, and decided roughly what you will grow, spring bulbs, summer annuals or whatever. Now comes the time to put the box in place and fill it, and how you tackle this may be between you and your osteopath. Ideally it would be nice to clear a space outside or put down a good layer of newspapers and work on the kitchen floor. The crunch comes however when you come to lift the box or to manoeuvre it into place on the window ledge. It may be just too heavy.

The alternative is to put the empty box in place and then fill it, but this may be awkward or time-consuming if you are working from steps outside, or from inside the room. Consider then the compromise: half fill the box in comfort and add the remaining compost and plants when it is *in situ.* What you use to fill your box must be something between you and your conscience rather than you and your bank manager. All that, just for a bag of dirt? is a common reaction to a hefty bill for compost and you may be tempted to thin the mix with garden soil, or even use garden soil alone. Now if you were cooking a meal and had added up the price of the ingredients you might be appalled, but you wouldn't consider replacing them with some cheap alternative. So grit your teeth and suffer the initial cost of good compost. It won't have to be changed every time you replant. When you take out the spring bulbs, for instance, and are ready to plant the summer annuals, you can simply top up with fresh compost. Add bonemeal, Growmore, or other inorganic fertilizer, mix it all around well and the new plants will do fine so long as you feed them regularly with liquid feed as well.

When you come to buy compost you will see that some kinds are gritty and soil-like and greyish and others are a deeper peaty brown and contain no stones. The first are usually identified as John Innes composts of which there are basically two, one for seed sowing and another for potting. Within the potting composts there are three different types, John Innes 1, 2, and 3, and you may also see another one labelled Ericaceous, which you need for acid-lovers like azaleas and rhododendrons.

John Innes is not a brand name, but a standard formula. The seed compost has a light, free-draining

structure so that it keeps warm and free of the excess moisture that could cause newly emerging roots to rot. Seed composts are low in nutrients, because seeds already contain their own essential nutrients. Potting compost is more moisture-retentive because by the time you come to repot plants their roots are better developed, more thirsty and less likely to rot. The difference between 1, 2, and 3 is simply the amount of base fertilizer. A window box to contain hardy or half hardy annuals growing steadily throughout the summer should be filled with JI 3, but it is as well to remember that this mix is a bit strong for repotting a cutting that you might have taken early in the season. Although in theory plants take what they want out of the soil, they can be harmed by an over-rich mix.

When first introduced, the John Innes soil-based composts revolutionized the world of window boxes by providing a reliable mix in which plants would flourish even in cramped conditions. Their disadvantages are that good turf loam, which is an essential ingredient, is now difficult to obtain and different brands of JI compost vary in quality. Having said that, I would still recommend a soil-based JI compost for use in a tub, planter or box standing on the ground or anywhere where weight is not a problem. Soil-based composts seem to me to dry out less than soilless, and are easier to rewet if this becomes necessary. A tip to remember if you are trying to water a dried-out compost is to add a few drops of washing-up liquid (mild liquid soap) to the water. But don't do this too often.

For window sills where weight is a factor, the development of soilless composts has itself been revolutionary. These are peat based and supplied with nutrients in varying strengths just like soil-based composts, but the trend today is towards multi-purpose composts that can be used for seed sowing, raising cuttings and the growing of established plants. The inclusion of vermiculite makes for an open structure that keeps a supply of water in the compost but allows excess to drain away. If the claims of these new multi-purpose composts sound a bit too all-embracing—good on toast, also kills rats—then I can only say that they do seem to do what they claim. But plants that have been repotted, or seedlings that have put on good roots, soon exhaust the available nutrients and should be regularly fed. Tap out any plant that has been in its pot for six weeks of growing weather and examine the root system. If it is vigorous, then start applying your chosen proprietary food at its recommended strength and intervals.

Judging how much soil-based or soilless compost you will need for your boxes and planters is not easy. Today bags of compost are commonly sold in small, economy, large, giant or jumbo packs. My favourite soilless seed and potting compost in its economy size comes in a bag that stands nearly 3 feet high and that I can lift only with difficulty. Nevertheless it is cheaper *pro rata* than its other sizes and lasts me well through the spring sowing and potting season. If you have room to store compost, do buy it in quantity; you will invariably find you need more than you think and it is infuriating to run out halfway through. If you should do so, don't top up with garden soil. This is always full of weed seeds—the composts you buy have

been sterilized to kill these—and tends to settle into a compacted state in any container, especially after it has been watered for a while. This is because in the open garden it is constantly being turned over by worms and other forms of insect life that only infrequently find their way into boxes, and this keeps it open and airy.

Different composts vary in bulk, which makes it difficult to give exact requirements for filling boxes and tubs. I find that one household bucket of soilless compost comfortably fills two plastic boxes, each $17 \times 5\frac{1}{2} \times 4$ inches (probably the smallest useful size for an outdoor box).

When buying compost for filling containers such as tubs or urns it is quite easy to make a mental comparison between their size and that of the ordinary household bucket. One bucket comfortably fills a terracotta pot 10 inches tall and 14 inches in diameter because, of course, the bottom couple of inches are filled with broken brick to give drainage. Remember the drainage layer, too, when calculating the amount you will need for filling boxes.

Hanging baskets should be filled as full of compost as possible. To look their best they have to be packed tight with plants and at the end of the season,

A layer of coarse peat prevents compost being washed through to the bottom layer of stones and brick.

when you come to turn them out, you can see just how crowded the roots are. Putting in the maximum growing medium is therefore essential; you will feed a basket regularly, of course, but the roots must have somewhere to spread. Planting a basket successfully is easy when you know how. The best way to keep it stable while you are planting is to rest it on top of a bucket standing on a table. This is a convenient height for working and also enables you to gauge the effect from below, as it will most often be seen. Some sort of liner is essential to enclose the compost and keep it from falling through the wire. Ideally this should be sphagnum moss, which is usually sold by the bag in the spring. It is expensive but, to my mind, preferable to black plastic or those discs of foam rubber now sold for the purpose. If you do use plastic, pierce it in a few places around the sides to allow plants to grow through; the foam discs are made with slits at the side for the same purpose.

No drainage layer of stones is necessary—the problem with baskets is usually to keep the water in, not out—so you can start filling compost directly on the moss or plastic lining. Insert plants to trail through the sides as you go, lying them on the sides and pulling the top growth through the holes very gently, then covering the roots with a further layer of compost. Trailing plants like lobelia soon adjust to this horizontal existence and it is much easier to plant as you go than to try and ram things in afterwards.

Larger plants, still in their pots, should again be arranged in position as you go along. Pack compost down well and water it—it will drop a little so you can add more—then it is a simple matter to slip the plants out of their pots and back into their neat holes without disturbing the roots. Fill any spaces left on the surface of the basket with wisps of trailing plants,

Support the hanging basket on a bucket while planting it up.

28

such as lobelia, or tuck in a few cuttings of tradescantia from indoors. This will grow quite well out of doors in the summer and can be thrown away at the end of the season. Ivy also roots well from cuttings, although it will make less top growth in only one season. If you can separate the roots when you come to break the basket up at the end of summer you could repot the new plants and bring them indoors.

Water, water and more water is what brings about the best blooming baskets, so before hanging one in some inaccessible spot think how you can best reach it—in very hot weather this may have to be three times a day, remember. Very often the easiest solution is to lengthen the chains so that the basket hangs at a more convenient height for watering.

Once a week a basket should be given a good dunking in a bucket of water. Settle it in position if you can so that it is just under the water level. Air bubbles will escape immediately and you should leave the basket immersed until these stop. If the basket is too wide for complete immersion, or if you are worried about damaging plants growing through the sides, take it down anyway, settle it carefully over a bucket and water gently and

persistently until the compost is nicely wet.

What with all the watering and the drying out and the dripping I am sometimes tempted to wonder whether hanging baskets are worth the trouble, although I have not yet had the heart to throw mine out. Growing well, they do make a splendid show and take up no valuable window sill, balcony or patio space at all. Currently I am trying out a solid plastic hanging basket that calls itself the Rolls-Royce of hanging baskets and comes as a completely sealed pot with a raised platform inside and a filling tube and water-level indicator. You water and feed through the tube when the indicator is low, which means that it is virtually self-watering. It sounds the ideal choice for anyone who can't water regularly and, as it is sealed, it should be safe enough to hang by the front door without dripping all over the step. But what happens if it rains hard on an already full reservoir I have yet to find out.

Other solid plastic hanging baskets incorporate a drip-tray to cut down on both drips and watering. Some of these are a bit ugly, at least until they are well furnished with plants, but I find them ideal for pendulous begonias. One tuber to a small basket and it soon becomes filled with greenery and, once flowering starts, is hardly seen.

GROWING FOR YOUR BOX

RAISING YOUR OWN PLANTS FROM SEEDS

The simplest way to fill window boxes and containers is to buy ready grown plants, annuals raised for summer bedding and perennials or biennials that are usually treated as annuals for a spring display.

Unfortunately the plants produced by commercial growers come from seed that is easy to raise and has a high percentage of germination and this tends to result in the more everyday colours and varieties. The plants, too, are usually brought to saleable condition—this often means in flower—rather too early in order to prolong the selling season. This gives customers the choice of buying early and then having to hang on to the plants somehow until the frosts are over, during which period they are liable to become starved of food and, more importantly, light. Alternatively, they can leave the plants in the garden centre for a week or two, but it is likely that even there they will become straggly if the spring is a late one. Because labour is expensive and watering not done as frequently as it should be the plants, already forced into premature flower, suffer even

further setback. In the open garden this is not such a problem; the plants will settle in a week or two and then start to flower. But the window box is no place for recuperating plants, and in the early summer particularly you want burgeoning flower, not sulking greenery.

What all this is leading up to is that you should choose ready raised plants with extreme care, buying if you can direct from the grower, who will advise you when it is safe to plant out in a window box. This is usually around the end of May, or early June; or from two to three weeks later in cold northern districts. Choose strong green plants, without flower but hopefully with signs of bud and without great tangles of root coming out of the bottom of the box. Remember that flowers sold cheaply in street markets and supermarkets are often those that have been rejected by other more demanding outlets; you may have to pay for your 'bargain' by waiting weeks for it to flower.

The alternative is, of course, to raise your own plants at home, and it has to be said at once that getting them to germinate is usually as easy as it

claims to be on the seed packet. It is getting them to grow after this that can prove a problem, unless you have lengths of very well lit window sill and don't mind living with seedboxes from February or March until the end of May. Then, providing you have a bit of sunny space outside where you can move plants in the daytime to get the light and air they need, you can have the exciting new colours and varieties that you won't yet find on sale. Seed companies, because they want you to succeed with their products, often give some indication of how easy each particular variety is to grow, marking the packet 'Germination: easy' or 'Germination: some experience necessary'. Some seeds are notoriously

difficult to raise, even for the expert, and where it admits that some experience is necessary it may well mean that the seeds need chilling in the fridge or over the winter, must be grown with bottom heat or in close conditions or even temperature, and that even then you may be rewarded with only a few plants.

Marigolds, which will seed all over the garden year after year without any attention from you, or forget-me-nots, honesty and many other old-fashioned cottagey plants are definitely in the easy category. Geraniums are more difficult. I never have much luck with seed and as it is expensive— especially for some of the new varieties—I usually rely on cuttings for new stock. Bottom heat helps bring most, but not all, seeds on and electric propagators of all sizes are now widely sold. These, if they can be regulated to provide a constant temperature of 65–70 °F, are extremely useful. The clear plastic tops, which should be wiped free of moisture every morning to let the maximum light in, help maintain an even humidity while the seeds are germinating; they are usually removed once the first shoots are visible so as to admit more light. Plastic seedboxes with clear plastic domes but without a heating element are also suitable for window sill

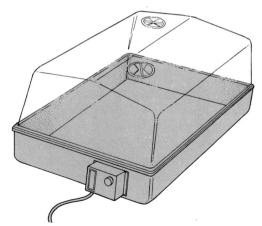

An electric propagator, complete with clear plastic lid, provides the bottom heat which gets seeds and cuttings away to a good start.

use. If you have radiators or storage heaters with wide enough tops, you can stand boxes on these to take advantage of the heat; without bottom heat there should still be germination but it will be slower. Mini-greenhouses and plant starters that come with compartmented seed trays standing on drip-trays and covered with clear domes are also very good, as the individual compartments allow a good root system to develop.

Seed packets seem to contain far less than they used to, but even the little pinch you get is usually more than enough for the average garden, let alone for window boxes. Open the vacuum packet or the pack inside carefully so as not to spill the contents and if the seed inside seems very small—as is the case with begonias and calceolarias—then mix it in the palm of your hand with a pinch of dry sand. This will help to disperse it more widely. A general purpose, soilless seed and potting compost is the best choice for indoor work as it seems to make less mess if spilt, but even for greenhouse use I still find this type encourages a better root system. You can use a conventional seedbox, standard size 14 × 9 inches or half size $8\frac{3}{4} \times 6\frac{1}{4}$ inches, and for these plastic domes are made to fit. But for starting seeds off, particularly if you perhaps want only a couple of

dozen plants, you can use a small half-pan flower-pot or a margarine tub provided with drainage holes in the bottom. The oblong-shaped margarine containers are particularly useful, as they can be fitted more neatly into a standard seed tray with dome. Sow one variety per tub. Mixed varieties will probably germinate at different rates and while pricking out one you will disturb the others. Sow seed thinly, taking up a pinch between the fingers and distributing it as evenly as you can right across the container and not just in the middle. Where seed is large enough set it out in individual stations; if you are sowing into individual compartments put two or three seeds in each and take out all but the strongest one when they come through. Follow the packet instructions as to depth of sowing; this is important.

Soilless composts tend to dry out quickly, although the best ones include a wetting agent to help retain moisture. So don't open bags before you need to, and squash out the air and reseal them to keep the remaining compost moist until you need it again. Fill containers to the rim, but don't compress down as the first watering will do this for you. Sink the pots into water up to just below their rims and leave them until moisture appears on the surface. Leave to

drain, cover and set in heat, if possible. Reserve the water which drains from the pot and use it for subsequent watering, as it contains useful nutrients. Incidentally, a not too hot airing cupboard is a good spot for starting seeds off, as long as you inspect the boxes regularly and remove them to light at the first signs of life. Shoots that continue to grow in the dark will be blanched and spindly and will probably never make good plants, so if this does happen it is better to throw them out and start again.

Don't rely on memory alone when you are raising seeds, especially if your freezer is like mine, full of Unidentified Frozen Objects I was sure I would remember again but can't. Label everything as you go, and as labels are wayward things and liable to become detached, I prefer to mark the side of the container with a chinagraph pencil. The mark will be permanent through waterings, but can be erased later with a cloth and scouring powder. Indicate the name of the plant and the date sown or, if the seed packet gives this, the date at which you should start to see growth. It also helps to keep pinned somewhere handy a record of what is sown and when, and how soon to expect germination, so that you know where you are with your seeds and whether you will have to augment with bought-in

plants. The chances are that you will. Because, though the newly sown seed may seem containable enough in its little margarine tubs, it will in a few weeks need pricking out into bigger boxes. One margarine tub of dahlia seed can produce fifty strong seedlings, which is ten too many for a large seedbox, so at a stroke your need for window sill space goes up from $5 \times 3\frac{1}{2}$ inches to 14×9 inches. Multiply this by the number of margarine tubs you sow and you can see how your elegant rooms are going to look like potting sheds before long.

And then there is the question of those extra ten, or probably more, seedlings. It seems such a shame to waste them, cruel even to leave them to die. So they get planted in a corner of another box that needs another bit of window sill. . . .

If all this sounds off-putting, it is certainly not meant to be. For many gardeners raising new plants is the most interesting job of all. If you are sowing your first seeds indoors, simply bear in mind the problems of getting sufficient light to young plants and the time needed to turn boxes and move them about so that plants don't develop a sideways list, to say nothing of taking them outdoors on warm days as they become larger and stronger.

The needs of the window sill plant raiser are

increasingly being met, not only with mini-greenhouses and electric propagators but also with seed starter kits. Just how useful these are varies considerably. Some come as small tubs filled with a growing medium such as vermiculite and are ready planted with seeds. You peel off the lid, sink the tub in water to water it and away you go.

Unfortunately, in transport the seeds often slide to one end of the container and germinate on top of one another instead of tidily throughout the tub. Other kits provide a rather flimsy seedbox and a bag of dust-dry compost that takes hours of soaking before it becomes moist enough to sow the seeds. Then when you have done that you realize that the seed tray has no holes in the bottom, so you struggle to make these without disturbing the newly sown seed . . . and spill the lot like as not. Even worse are the kits that offer you mixed selections of seed that germinate at different rates. By and large you can do better—and more cheaply—with a recycled margarine tub and a conveniently small-sized pack of compost, plus a pack of seeds of course.

The new all-purpose seed and potting composts are well supplied with nutrients and trace elements that are intended to last the plants, and particularly seedlings, for a certain length of time. Judging when to begin feeding newly raised plants is not too difficult, even though it is important not to overfeed. As a general rule, newly emerged seedlings do not need feeding as you will be pricking them out into fresh compost as soon as they are large enough to handle. You can start feeding pricked-out seedlings that are growing away well after three to six weeks. The size and the rate of growth of the plant are the things to go by; if seedlings start to romp away then they are using up nutrients and these should be replaced once a week with a watering in of plant food at the recommended strength for seedlings (usually half that for fully established plants). If newly pricked out seedlings are making little growth, they are probably still recovering from the shock of pricking out. Feeding would not stir them into activity, so delay this until they have started to make growth. You can overfeed plants, and the resulting overconcentration of nutrients in the soil will actually check growth; be guided by the growth rate.

The shock to a tiny seedling of being uprooted and transferred to another box is not as traumatic as one might think. Obviously you take great care, holding the tiny plant by its seed leaves—the first ones to appear and usually different from its adult leaves—and not by the main shoot. You lift it carefully out of its original home and drop it equally carefully into a hole made for it in a tray of fresh compost. A half tray will usually take twenty plants and a full-size tray forty to fifty. Drop the seedling into the hole right up to its seed leaves. Planting too shallow makes for spindly plants that keel over when you water them, so drop them well down into the new compost.

Seedlings need as much light as they can get but should be protected from strong sunlight for a few

Hold the seedling by its seed leaves.

days after pricking out. Turn the boxes daily to encourage plants to grow up straight, water with a fine spray so as not to knock them right over. And watch the weather. Spring, when the bulk of seedlings are being raised, is a time of widely fluctuating temperatures, from below freezing at night to anything from 70 °F upwards during the day. In a centrally heated house a window sill temperature is unlikely to reach freezing at night, but with the sun on it at midday it can easily reach 80 or 90 °F. It is not a bad idea to hang a room thermometer near the windows to check the temperature variations during this critical time.

Most of the plants you will want to sow for your window box will be pretty tough and able to cope with a bit of rough treatment. Certainly they won't want cosseting. But careful treatment will ensure maximum growth in minimum time, rewarding you with sturdy plants that can be planted out just when you need them.

RAISING YOUR OWN PLANTS FROM CUTTINGS

To look at the price of plants in the shops you would never believe how easy many of them are to raise from cuttings. You have to pay, of course, for the

35

grower's time and for his heating bills as well as his expertise, so it is unfair to begrudge him his price. But if you are prepared to spend a little time, and have access to cuttings material—this does not mean rampaging around the local park or botanical garden with a sharp knife and a plastic bag—you can soon build up a quantity of plants for almost nothing.

Geraniums and fuchsias are good examples of plants that are expensive to buy and easy to propagate from cuttings taken at almost any time of the year when the plant is in growth. From the geranium of your choice, and preferably with its owner's permission, take off an ideally but not necessarily non-flowering shoot about 4–6 inches long. Strip off the lower leaves, leaving just two or three, and slice the stem neatly between the nodes, that is between the raised lumps at which leaves are attached to the stem. Use a sharp knife or razor blade to get a clean cut—ragged tears encourage disease—and dip the end into hormone rooting powder. You can manage without this and most of us had to before it was invented, but it does speed up the growth of roots. Tap off the excess powder, and drop the cutting into a hole made for it close to the edge of a compost-filled flower-pot. You can get three or four around the edge of a 3½ inch

flower-pot and more around a large half pan; cuttings should be not too closely touching and always seem to root faster if planted around the sides of the pot. Water from below and keep 'close', which means cover with a plastic dome or even with a plastic bag hood secured to the pot with a rubber band; this is known as a Wisley pot and means that you may never again be able to throw away a used plastic bag. Try not to let leaves touch the plastic and shake off excess moisture daily as too damp an atmosphere will encourage the growth of moulds.

After a week or so you can open up the vent in the plastic dome or snip off a corner of the plastic bag, then a week later, if all looks well, remove the cover altogether. Your cuttings will need full daylight and bottom heat if at all possible and must not be allowed to become dry. In four to six weeks, depending on the time of year, you should see new leaves forming at the tip of the plant, and this indicates that roots have formed. Not too long after this joyful discovery you can repot the plants in individual 3½ inch pots. Do this carefully, up-ending the cuttings, holding the top of the pot with widespread fingers and tapping the bottom to dislodge the compost ball. If your pot was clean and dry when you planted it, and if the compost has not been

Dip the end of the cutting in hormone rooting powder to encourage root development.

allowed to dry out, it will come out cleanly and you will be able to separate the individual plants carefully. Settle them into their new pots, firming down very gently, water and keep them somewhere warm and light but out of direct sun for a few days. A 100 per cent germination rate might be a bit optimistic, but unless you have gone drastically wrong somewhere you should get 75 per cent with geraniums. Cuttings taken in August and September and overwintered on an inside window sill could be flowering by spring. But for summer blooms, take out buds as they appear and direct the plant's energy into making strong root and stem growth. Once roots start to appear at the drainage hole the plant is ready for potting in a 5 inch pot. In spring, regular feeding with a proprietary feed will be necessary. Plants will sometimes struggle on for months with no more than the nutrients that compost supplies. But give them some extra food and see how they romp away.

Fuchsias are propagated in the same way. As with geraniums, August and September are the months for taking cuttings and getting optimum success and this certainly coincides with the need to make new plants for next year's display. But if you are offered a cutting of any likely plant during the growing season always take it and give it a try.

The summer months are the time to take softwood cuttings (as above). Hardwood cuttings are usually taken in October, from the current year's growth of shrubs. Lengths of leafless stem, from 4 to 12 inches long, are inserted along a sandy trench of about a spade's depth, and this may be all a bit much for a window box gardener. But leave a few sprigs of forsythia or flowering currant in water for a few weeks and you may well see roots begin to break at the base, even in the spring. Plant them carefully in soilless compost in deepish containers such as the 10 ounce ones for cream or yoghurt, look after them and you may well have a tidy plant by autumn. Ivy will also throw out roots in water and this is an economical way of furnishing the fronts of boxes with trailing ivy.

If you get the propagation bug badly you will need more detailed information than there is room to give here. Hanker after camellias from cuttings, or bay, or azaleas or magnolias and you may find you are in a different ball-game. But there is never any harm in trying, for hope is what we all live on.

Cuttings should not touch closely. A plastic bag tied round the pot will prevent cuttings from drying out before rooting starts.

37

Rosemary

Hebe 'Pagei'

Juniperus communis 'Compressa'

Picea abies pumila

Senecio
cineraria

Crocus
tomasinianus

Hedera helix
'Goldheart'

Boxes from Outside the House

THE ALL-SEASON BOX

Compared to the great splashes of colour that can be achieved by the well-planted summer and spring box, the all-season box is but a pale shadow. Nevertheless, it is the right choice for many people. If you travel a lot in business, and so cannot guarantee the regular watering that a more colourful flowering box requires, or if you like to seal up the windows at the first sign of a cold snap and don't want to open them again for watering until spring, you can set your sights a little lower. A box of ivy and conifer may not stop passers-by in their tracks but it can create a bit of interest throughout the year. Then, when the travel programme slows down or the weather brightens up, you can use this as the framework for more exciting seasonal displays.

Ivy is a most accommodating plant. Indoors you may not have found it so, and this is probably because you keep your rooms fairly warm and consequently very dry. In these conditions it will sulk or shrivel but the same plant, cast out as not worth the space it is taking up, can romp away in the open garden or in any kind of container out of doors.

Conifers vary in their adaptability, but there are so many from which to choose that you can usually find specimens suitable for boxes and tubs even in the least well-stocked shops and garden centres. Since there is such an enormous choice, it is worth shopping a little farther afield, if you have to, to find a tree that has an interesting shape, or unusual foliage, or both. Either way it is important to choose the conifer that has been correctly bred for growing in a small space. Miniature means different things to different growers, so try to find a helpful assistant when you buy, to reassure you that your purchases really are suitable for window box planting.

Chimney pots can be planted with dwarf conifers, ivy, hebe or rosemary to make a display which has year-round interest. Crocuses can be planted for a splash of colour in the spring while roses would look lovely in the summer. But don't mix this sort of permanent planting with floppy bedding annuals; stick to shrubs of more rigid form.

A few preconceived ideas will do no harm but as a general rule it is unwise to be too specific about the dwarf conifers you want. Certain well-known varieties are offered by good nurseries all over the country but others are less easily obtainable. Maybe they have proved to have a drawback, and commercial growers have stopped producing them and switched to some more amenable variety of similar appearance. Fashions come and go in nursery stock just as in other things, and it is no good insisting on this particular juniper or fir any more than it is any good demanding winkle-pickers if the world and his wife are into clumpy shoes.

It is worth knowing a few names, however, to give your helpful assistant some idea of the kind of plant you are looking for. *Juniperus communis* 'Compressa', for instance, is a slow-growing blueish green juniper that has neat upright growth and is very suitable for window boxes and containers with its eventual height of 2 feet and spread of 6 inches. It is very widely available and can sometimes even be found in chain store garden sections. *Chamaecyparis pisifera* 'Boulevard' is another easy-to-find subject. Its colour is a steely blue seemingly tipped with white and its shape is more lax and feathery.

Juniperus communis 'Prostrata' reaches little more than 12 inches in height but can spread to 5 feet; *J. horizontalis* has a number of named varieties whose habit is prostrate but that are easy to keep pruned. *Picea abies*, the Norway spruce, has a number of dwarf forms including 'Clanbrassiliana', which is a low, rounded bush when young and which grows so slowly that it can to all intents and purposes be regarded as dwarf. This perhaps prompts the question: could not any conifer be used as background material until it grew too big, when it could be removed to the open garden or even the dustbin? The answer is a guarded yes, but with certain provisos. Conifers, other than the fast-growing hedging varieties, can be expensive to buy and you may feel that you are paying too much for a tree that is to be thrown out after a year or two. There is also the danger that the drastically constricted roots will expand and crack an expensive container. These roots will also starve anything else growing nearby. And, finally, the more expensive dwarf varieties are dwarf in all their particulars; they are true miniatures with mini branches, mini needles and, though infrequently, mini cones. Small young specimens of forest trees lack this delicacy. I have a seedling of a Leyland cypress; the parent stands in the garden at a current 20 feet and could well make

50 feet one day, while junior stands a mere 6 inches and is confined in a yoghurt container until I can think where to plant him. Meanwhile it has to be said that he lacks decorative appeal in his small plastic home; I certainly wouldn't want him in a window box.

Ivy—hedera in the nurseryman's catalogue—is widely available and relatively inexpensive. It also roots fairly easily, even in water, so that you can take cuttings of a variety you admire, choosing shoots where the plant characteristics—heavily notched or brightly variegated leaves—are most intense. Plants to buy for a box include *Hedera canariensis*, which has leathery leaves and varieties splotched with cream or silver grey. *H.c.* 'Variegata' has dark green centres and silver grey or white borders. *Canariensis* varieties will climb or trail, their only drawback being a rather larger leaf than other ivies. *Hedera helix* is the common ivy of trees and hedgerows; you could plant it in a box or tub but would do better with some of its more interesting forms such as 'Buttercup' (also offered as 'Russell's Gold' or 'Golden Cloud'), which is a really bright golden colour, 'Glacier' with small silver grey and white leaves, 'Goldheart' with small narrow leaves and bright gold central markings, or some of the

sagittaefolia forms like 'Tricolor', which turns from green and white in summer to a deep rose in the autumn. Variegated ivies keep their colours best in a south or west facing box; in a shady place the colours dim. Green shoots should be removed as soon as they are noticed or they will take over.

Some ivies have a marked tendency to climb. 'Goldheart' is one; it grows stiffly upwards or straight along the soil and I can never persuade it to trail. Others will trail nicely over the front of the box but will need a bit of encouragement if you also want them to go upwards. If wooden trellis would be too heavy in appearance, or too difficult to secure, you could use strings of wire or fillis, tied around nails driven into the wall (if possible) or window surround (if this is easier). The string should be fairly tight against the wall so that it supports the shoot until it makes its own anchorage.

Early spring is the time to prune ivy back to its support and then again in summer if any shoots grow too long. When the plant is young resist the temptation to let it run to a few very long shoots and cut them back to encourage more shoots to break from lower down.

You could plant a box with, say, three conifers, not necessarily all the same but sharing the same

blue-green or yellow-green shades, two upright and one more prostrate. Then add a couple of small ivies, again in the same colour range as the trees—mixing leaf shades is rarely successful in a small planting like a window box and a variety of plants sharing the same green spectrum has much more impact. This would provide interest all year, although more in the summer perhaps when the variegations show more brilliantly or the spring when the new tips of both ivy and conifers appear delicately green. Hebes are evergreen shrubs certain of which are ideal for the year-round container. H. 'Pagei' is one of the hardiest—hebes mostly hail from New Zealand and can be cut down by frost but I have always found this one a survivor. Its height may be no more than 9 inches and its spread about 2—3 feet, the shape is nicely rounded, the leaves glaucous and the small white flower spikes show in May and June. H. albicans has a height and spread of about 2 feet, longer leaves and again glaucous leaves and white flowers. H. × franciscana 'Variegata' has leaves marked with cream and admittedly rather wishy-washy mauve flowers, but it is tough and looks well in window boxes where the variegated leaves are seen to advantage.

Hebes come in a great many different forms,

some reaching as much as 5 feet, so you should be certain of your variety—or at least its eventual size—before buying. On the other hand, I find hebes ridiculously easy to root from cuttings taken in July or August. These plants should be ready to pot the following spring and by autumn would be large enough to go in an all-season planting. Judicious picking out of shoots would keep them neat for a year or two (although this might deprive you of some flowers). As 'freebies' they could be thrown out when too big, or potted as gifts for garden-owning friends or donations to local charity plant stalls. Nor would it be difficult to keep a supply of replacement plants coming.

Senecio is another shrub that is easily rooted from cuttings. In the open ground it soon gets straggly and is best replaced with freshly raised plants every few years. S. laxifolius has light grey leaves thickly covered with white felt. The flowers are yellow daisies and many gardeners pick them off at bud stage, preferring the plant for its foliage effects, but I think I might keep them in a window box display. S. bicolor, still sold as Cineraria maritima, is a pretty hardy evergreen sub-shrub that would blend well with the larger S. laxifolius. You can raise this easily from seed or buy plants in spring.

They flop a bit in the very cold weather or if they are allowed to dry out too much but are generally easygoing. For a little extra interest in the spring I would have *Crocus tomasinianus* in a form such as 'Whitewell Purple', only 3 inches high with small wide-open purple faces and vastly superior to the large flowering types. Cotoneaster is not often chosen for window boxes though you may see it in those large planters used to break the monotony of paved areas in cities. The evergreen varieties are obviously best for a year-round display. *C. congestus* may reach no more than 6 inches high and spread up to 3 feet with tiny pink flowers in June and bright red berries in winter. *C. horizontalis* is the fishbone cotoneaster you see trained up walls and showing bright red berries, but few leaves, in winter; it is vigorous and easygoing.

Lonicera includes our old friend the honeysuckle, Shakespeare's woodbine. Since it roots vigorously you should be able to scrounge a cutting or buy a small plant quite cheaply. The way to keep it neat and furnished down to soil level with leaves rather than the 30 foot crown of leaves and blossom on the end of a 6 foot bare brown stem, which is how it grows in the garden, is to keep cutting out the tips of vigorous shoots. This encourages growth low down and means that you will not need to prune hard back and lose all the flowers. Honeysuckle needs something to twine around, so fix wires or strings and help shoots along by winding them around these rather than letting them twine around one another. *L. japonica* is evergreen and has fragrant flowers in summer, *L. periclymenum* is the native English honeysuckle, so more correctly the flower of Shakespeare; it is richly fragrant but deciduous.

Rosemary is a plant more commonly associated with the kitchen herb box but a well-shaped plant makes a good subject for an all-season box, with the added bonus of an occasional source of flavour for cooking. *R. officinalis* has spikes of pale mauve flowers in spring and then sporadically throughout the summer, 'Albiflorus' has white flowers, 'Erectus' a more upright pyramid shape. *R. o. prostatus* I find a bit of a sulker, trailing so far and then stopping, or even succumbing entirely in a very cold winter. In a window box it might do better; with its light green leaves and pale blue flowers it is certainly worth a try, especially in a city, where temperatures are always higher. Keep rosemary in shape by judicious tipping of shoots, which you will want to do anyway for the kitchen. In front of rosemary I would plant thyme, especially the lemon-scented *Thymus* ×

citriodorus 'Silver Queen', and keep this trim, too, by picking off tips for cooking. Once again for a spring show I would want to plant small bulbs, such as species crocus in blue or purple or white, or muscari, blue or white or tiny blue squills. It is all too easy, you see, to stray from your original intention of planting a low-maintenance year-round background of well selected greens and to want to introduce bits of seasonal colour. Bulbs, certainly, are low maintenance but you cannot expect them to come up smiling year after year in the confines of a box. Having said that, some will, for it is in the nature of plants to confound those who dare pronounce on them. But popping in a few new bulbs each autumn is not too arduous a task; if, when the flowers are over you are bothered by the untidy foliage lift the bulbs out and try to find a home for them in open ground.

The other way to add seasonal spice to an all-season box is to drop in pot-grown specimens in flower. To make this even easier sink empty 3½ inch pots into spaces between the permanent plants— the foliage will soon grow over the holes—and take these out only when you have a new flowering occupant. This means primroses or polyanthus in early spring, pansies in winter and spring, or maybe something showy such as a cineraria in the summer. But on the whole these all-season displays do not mix well with the exuberant annuals of summer, so resist the temptation to tuck in marigolds or geraniums or almost any of the familiar summer bedding plants. Neat fibrous-rooted begonias, perhaps—when the first frost threatens these can be removed, cut back and potted to make indoor flowers throughout next winter and spring. Or you might try a few impatiens, especially those with a leaf colour that is sympathetic to the rest of the arrangement; some of the bronze-leaved varieties are attractive even when not in flower.

If the urge for summer colour overcomes you, you might do better to plant another box and do a quick swap when the annuals have settled down and begun to make a show. The all-season box can then go in some out-of-the-way spot where it will still have light and water throughout the summer, perhaps even plunged in a friend's garden. A less drastic step, perhaps, than giving up your jet-setting job in favour of one that is easier to structure around the lifestyle of your window boxes.

THE SEASONAL BOX

SPRING

Corny it may be, but there is no more heart-warming sight to a gardener than the emerging spikes of the first spring bulbs. If you plant your bulbs early in boxes of good peaty compost—not bulb fibre, some of which is about as much good as sawdust—you should see the first signs of growth soon after Christmas. As I write (in early March) I have snowdrops and crocus, both the tiny species crocus, which I prefer, and the big fat hybrids, which I like less but have to admit are a welcome splash of colour just now. Then there are *Eranthis hyemalis*, the winter aconite, which has buttercup flowers surrounded by a frilly ruff of leaves as early as February and so is beginning to go over now, and chionodoxa, which have blue, pink or white star-shaped flowers; *C. gigantea* reaches 8 inches in height and has large pale violet-blue flowers with a paler centre and *C. luciliae* 'Alba' reaches 5 inches and has white flowers. The pink form *C. luciliae* 'Pink Giant' reaches 6 inches; it is not always easy to get hold of but worth growing if you can find it.

I have also *Anemone blanda*, with its low-growing lilac pink or white daisy-like flowers; this does well in the light soil of my garden, where I set it out after it has first provided me with a solid mat of colour in a shallow pan beside the kitchen door. Then in April there will be muscari in blue and white, species iris, of which more later as this is a very large and diverse group, and our old friends the daffodils, hyacinths and tulips, which nevertheless must be selected with care if they are to look their best in a window box.

Being set loose among the bulb selections in the local garden centre is like being a child again in a sweet shop. There are so many to choose from and, if you are to believe all you read about them, each promises such a combination of colour, fragrance, quality and abundance of flowering that the only problem would seem to be how to stop the whole thing looking frightfully vulgar.

Alas, horticulture has its own hyperbole and one man's charming and outstanding variety with bright orange-scarlet flowers forming a vivid contrast to the glossy apple green foliage, etc, etc, etc, may be your damp squib. You will fare no better among the

bulb catalogues, either, because here there is even more room for fantasizing. Catalogues, however, are a good source of information about varieties and when you have only a limited amount of space in which to achieve maximum effect it is important to choose your bulbs carefully. This is more easily done quietly at home than in the Sunday morning rush of the garden centre or the Friday night hell of the supermarket. To help you make up your mind, think hard about the effect you wish to create in your spring box. Is it maximum impact? Then snowdrops clearly are not the best choice, and a tight mass of hyacinths in a deep pink such as 'Pink Pearl' would be better.

Hyacinths have always been among the more expensive of the spring bulbs, and many people have given up trying to mass them in the open garden and keep them exclusively for growing in pots and boxes. Bulb growers, quick to see how the wind blows, have responded with more and more varieties that have the right characteristics for container growing. Most important of these is the ability to stand up straight. Unfortunately the flower trusses have been improved over and over again but the stems seem to have been neglected, with the result that a really beautiful specimen keels over almost as soon as the last flower bell has opened. This is a pity in a bedding scheme but a disaster in a window box. So look for varieties that claim a strong stem: 'Lady Derby', a late flowerer with pale shell pink flowers; 'Mme du Barry', a strong deep pink; 'L'Innocence', white; 'Jan Bos', another deep, nearly red pink; 'Tubergen's Scarlet', carmine; and 'Amsterdam', deep salmon. Among the yellows I like 'City of Haarlem', which is a primrose shade and so more unusual.

If a hyacinth is described as having 'graceful stems' or if the prose goes on about colour, compactness and fragrance only then I should leave it alone. If you must buy that variety, or if you have bought a strong-stemmed variety and the rotters still look like keeling over, the only course is to stake each flower truss. Use the thin green sticks sold for staking house plants and try to get them into the soil rather than through the bulb itself, unless you are not bothered about planting them in the garden later. Twist-ties make the neatest tie and should be kept loose enough not to restrict the passage of sap up the flower stem.

Daffodils are better seen in Wordsworthian hosts than in prim rows in the window box. Having said that, Wordsworth's hosts of golden daffodils were

A spring version of the instant box can have primroses and pansies tucked in between dwarf conifers and ivy. This makes an arrangement which is really easy-care, but if you have the time in September pop in some crocuses, muscari or tiny irises for an authentic touch of spring. Snowdrops do not come readily from dried bulbs. Try to buy them 'in the green' just after they have finished flowering and you will be more certain of success with these first harbingers of spring.

Thuja occidentalis
pygmaea

Viola x Williamsii
'Campanula Blue'

Chamaecyparis lawsoniana
'Tamariscifolia'

Viola x
Wittrockiana

Primula
vulgaris

Hedera helix
'Glacier'

Juniperus
taxifolia

not the splendidly perianthed, magnificently trumpeted specimens of today but *Narcissus pseudonarcissus*, the wild daffodil or Lent lily, which, though delightful, is pale by comparison and best seen *en masse*. I find daffodils in rows rather silly in the open garden, but acceptable in a window box and rather more than acceptable in a large tub or planter. The secret is to pack them in tightly to make a clump rather than a row. Daffodils start in size with miniatures such as the 6 inch *Triandrus albus* in creamy white and with petals swept back, or bulbocodium, which is all trumpet and very little perianth, also 6 inches, or the even tinier minimus, which is probably the smallest of all the trumpet daffodils at only 3 inches tall. These are all quite delightful if massed in a shallow pan or combined with rocks and miniature conifers in an alpine box but obviously unsuitable for a grand display.

At the other end of the size scale come the 20 inch whoppers like 'Belisana', which has a rich orange crown and white perianth, or 'Texas', which is a yellow and orange double. Even the somewhat overused 'King Alfred' comes out at 18 inches and this is the most usual size in popular varieties. To my mind this is a bit high for a window box unless you have a good tall window or have slung your box low

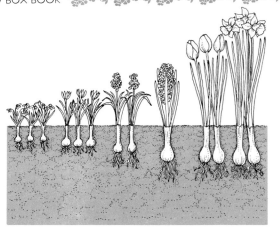

Plant bulbs at their recommended depths—the larger the bulb, the deeper in most cases, but not all.

so that plants won't blot out the light. Daffodil foliage can flop messily after a while but the flowers are usually carried erect so this is a point to be considered.

Slightly smaller in both height and size of flower are the dwarf cyclamineus narcissi. 'February Gold' (which never comes till March for me but is none the less welcomed for its long yellow frilled trumpets) grows to 12 inches, 'Peeping Tom' is another early-flowering variety at 14 inches, 'Suzy' is yellow and orange and 12 inches, and 'Jenny' is an all-white also at 12 inches. Bulbs in this division frequently produce two or three flowers each,

which helps the massed effect.

Double-flowering daffodils you either love or hate. It is currently fashionable to abhor them but I don't, and I would certainly choose them for box work provided the box was not too exposed to the wind, which beats down the rather heavy heads.

Yellow King Alfreds we have seen before, many, many times, but 'Irene Copeland', 14 inches, cream, has petals as tightly packed as a small dahlia or chrysanthemum and 'Tahiti', at 15 inches, has a mix of golden yellow petals with a smaller bright orange centre.

To the expert a daffodil is always a narcissus but we tend to think of narcissus as the short-trumpeted variety, such as the poeticus species with their white perianths and orange crowns. Rather than bother about the different divisions—bicolour large cups, jonquilla, triandrus and so on—select daffodils for a box entirely on the information you can get about them. Most bulbs are sold from open boxes, or in packs, with a good illustration and details of size and colour; don't fall for any with an incomplete description because although they may well be cheaper they cannot be guaranteed to provide the effect you want in a box. Daffodils should be planted early, in August if possible and certainly no later than early September if you aim for early flowering. Cover the bulbs with compost to one and a half times the depth of the bulb, measuring it from base to shoulder. This means a bulb measuring 2 inches from base to shoulder should be covered with 3–4 inches of soil. Failure with daffodils, indeed with most bulbs, can usually be put down to incorrect depth of planting.

Buy bulbs of equal size and fill your box to the correct depth to accommodate this size. Make the compost level, then stand the bulbs in place, only just not touching if you can manage it or touching lightly if it allows you to pack in a few more bulbs. Yes, I know that daffodils in the garden suffer from overcrowding and should be better spaced, but yours will only be in the box for one flowering. Then pour the remaining compost around the bulbs, firm, and water well. Don't do it the other way around, filling, then pushing the bulbs in to what you hope is the right depth. You will end up with compost all over the place and daffodils planted at uneven depths that will then not flower all together.

Tulips can be planted much later than most other bulbs so if you find you have left it a bit late you could put these in a window box. November is the best time to plant and even up till Christmas will do;

the bulb tips should be 4 inches below the surface of the compost, and despite the fact that we are always recommended to space them out in the garden I push them up much closer to get a bold effect. Tall tulips, like the Darwin and Darwin hybrids, are the tulips that grow as they are told in places other than Brooke's Grantchester. Better for boxes are the early doubles, around 12 inches, such as 'Marechal Niel' in orangey yellow with nice slightly frilled petals, or 'Jewel Dance', which is 11 inches and red tipped with white. A row of muscari 'Early Giant' along the front of the box will provide extra interest at the time of flowering. Even better are the fosteriana, greigii and kaufmanniana hybrids. These are among the earliest colour in the garden and do equally well in box or container; they have for me the added advantage of being much more dwarf and so looking less like tulips and more like waterlilies. The greigii hybrids, 'Red Riding Hood', 8 inches tall, 'Plaisir', 10 inches, red edged with sulphur yellow, 'Cheresade', 8 inches, scarlet with a black base, have beautifully mottled or veined leaves that are a picture in themselves even before the flowers come. 'Franz Lehar', 6 inches, is another wide-awake tulip in sulphur yellow with a deeper yellow throat that also has striped leaves, and

'Golden Eagle' is taller at 14 inches with deep yellow flowers, a scarlet flash on the outside and combining apricot, yellow, scarlet and black in a way to confuse the most ardent catalogue writer.

The tulip genus runs to some fifteen divisions, proving that tulipomania is certainly not dead. To make a choice even from the less expensive, more commonly available varieties it is probably best to write off for catalogues and spend a few happy hours choosing the combination of height, colour and habit that appeals to you most. Be tough with yourself and resist the temptation to mix varieties, unless you can keep them very separate. If you have a shallow dish or half pan, plant it tightly with 'Rockery Beauty', which has tiny blood-red pointed flowers and which will make a flat carpet of colour.

I have suggested muscari to make an edging for a box of tulips because this sort of mixing increases the impact rather than muddling it as a mixture of individual varieties does. But you will have to be careful in your mixing, and make sure that the two will flower together. Nothing is more disappointing than a brave show of muscari spikes fronting a mess of waning tulips.

This is why it is often best to buy from a specialist catalogue, rather than from a serve-yourself display.

When ordering, you can state that you want the flowers to come together and ask for another variety to be substituted if the grower himself thinks it safer. Or buy from a good nursery or garden centre when things are not too busy and you can find someone to advise you. Muscari, of course, are well worth growing in their own right. Plant them 3 inches deep and almost touching, since they are not to be left undisturbed. *M. tubergenianum* comes out in March or April and has spikes of graded blue, 8 inches, and 'Early Giant', 6 inches, has large flowers of a good blue. *M. botryoides* 'Album', 6 inches, comes in April and is white while *M. comosum* 'Plumosum' has feathery tufts of purple rather than the more familiar grape-shaped florets. This flowers later, in May.

I am a bit besotted with crocus, I don't think nearly enough use is made of the species such as *C. tomasinianus*, *C. chrysanthus* and *C. vernus*.

C. tomasinianus is an early flowerer, in February and early March; 'Barr's Purple' and 'Whitewell Purple' are deeper versions of the pale mauve type. At only 3 inches high, it needs massing in a shallow bowl or could be used to front a display of early daffodils, one of the dwarf cyclamineus like 'Dove Wings' or 'Jenny', both in creamy white.

C. chrysanthus has a hybrid 'Zwanenburg Bronze' that is bronze outside and yellow inside, while 'E. A. Bowles' is yellow with a bronze base. I would also choose 'Snow Bunting' for its pure white flowers and yellow centres or 'Cream Beauty'. Openness of habit is a feature of these small species, which means that a considerable number of bi- and tricolours have been bred. Again they look well in shallow bowls, either at ground level where you can look down into their open faces or closer to eye level—on a convenient wall or ledge by front or back door perhaps—where you can see them in close-up as you come and go. These smaller crocuses are the ones for me, and fortunately they can now be found in most garden centres. These usually have such a good selection that you should be able to find dozens to your liking. Once again, don't mix them, but plant them closely with about 3 inches of soil above their shoulders.

And now for those irises, of which there are some three hundred and a great many of which are totally unsuitable for box work. So forget the flag irises of the June border with their huge purple standards (the inner petals) and falls (the outer petals) each arranged in threes. Forget also the long-stemmed florists' iris and instead look among

the bulbous irises in the shops in the autumn. These include the low-growing *I. bakeriana* in a mix of pale and dark blue splotched with white. It reaches 6 inches and comes up in February and March. *I. danfordiae* is another early dwarf, this time yellow, as is *I. histrioides*, of which the most commonly found variety is 'Major' at 4 inches high and with deep blue flowers splashed with yellow in the centre. *I. reticulata*, 6 inches, comes in a range of blues: 'Harmony' is dark blue, 'Cantab' light blue, 'J. S. Dijt' a warm purple. A feature of these tiny irises is that they flower when the leaves are very immature and in some cases all but absent. Later the leaves can grow quite tall but by this time you will probably have planted them out in the garden. Whether they will flourish there is a matter of luck—*I. danfordiae* is never very robust—but it is always worth a try. Bulbous irises could be planted in a window box but I would rather see them in shallow containers— they need only be planted $2\frac{1}{2}$ inches deep—and close together for maximum impact. In a 12 inch pot I would plant a dozen of the tiny bulbs, then put them somewhere where they can be seen close up and also smelled.

If you love woodland bluebells, *Scilla non-scripta*, you would also enjoy some of the siberians,

S. sibirica, which comes along with the crocuses in March and stays at a neat 4 inches. Or try *S. tubergeniana*, another mini, with white or china blue bells. Again plant these close together in pans rather than in boxes.

Snowdrops, again for a shallow pan, come in an astonishing number of different varieties many of which can only be told apart by enthusiasts. The common snowdrop, *Galanthus nivalis*, can vary in height between 3 and 8 inches and another fairly easily obtained snowdrop, *G. elwesii*, is taller at 6–10 inches. The former flower from January and the latter February to March. The only snag with snowdrops is that many of those little white bulbs offered for sale in the autumn will never actually produce a flower. Plant a dozen and if you are very lucky you may get three up the first year and five years later be even luckier to discover that they like you and have established themselves from seed.

Since a failure rate of two out of three is unacceptable in container gardening you will have to buy your snowdrops 'in the green', that is as divisions of recently flowered clumps in spring. These are not often to be found in garden centres but specialist growers will supply them by post. This makes them more expensive, even for the very

common varieties. Don't go for the more unusual ones as these are not only very expensive but are also best left to the enthusiast who will jolly them along in the alpine house. Don't, please, dig up any you see growing in the wild; this is immoral and illegal. If you must plant bulbs do this as soon as you spot them on sale; the longer they are exposed to air the less successful they will be.

While shopping for spring-flowering bulbs you will undoubtedly see others I haven't mentioned. Erythroniums you could try, although they are rather expensive, *Fritillaria meleagris* you might fall for because of its delightful speckled bell flowers, but I have never got the brute to perform; *Allium moly*, which straggles in the garden, I once hoped would trail prettily out of a pot planted with a dwarf conifer. Well, it didn't, it straggled just as it does in the garden. The less common bulbs are naturally expensive and the chances are that they are for the specialist to grow in a cold frame or alpine house; it might be better if you want to be more sure of success to stick to the easier ones I have suggested. Having said that, of course, there is no reason to stick to plain old 'King Alfred' daffodils when you could have 'Mount Hood', an all-white trumpet variety, or the lovely double 'Van Sion' with its

thickly bunched centres and star-like perianth.

Autumn is the time for preparing the spring bulb box. Bulbs start to appear in the shops and garden centres in August and to be sure of getting the varieties you want it is often necessary to snap them up as soon as you see them. Not such a bad idea, if you can keep them in a cool, dry place—remember it's August—until September or in the case of tulips as late as November. If the retailer is managing his stock well he will have put them out in a cool area and in this respect some supermarkets are beautifully cool, not to say quite chilly, and so ideal for the storage of bulbs. Others, especially the chain stores and variety chains, get very hot, and bulbs that have languished in heat and under strong light for several weeks will not be in the peak condition in which they left the grower. Bulbs from specialist suppliers are ordered some time during the summer from spring-supplied catalogues and deliveries are usually made in the first week in September. This means the bulbs stay in optimum condition until immediately before posting, and if you get them into your box as soon as possible after arrival you can expect the best results. Better still, you can usually arrange to collect from the grower at the most convenient time for you. Having said all this, there is

no need to get neurotic about shop or garden centre bought bulbs. The majority of bulbs you see nodding away in gardens in the spring have come from these less than perfect sources and are none the worse for it. It is only that the demands of the window box garden are for perfect flowers, all arriving at the same time and all making the best possible show.

When you select bulbs from open displays choose those that feel firm and heavy with no signs of mould, soft patches or bruising. Loose skins are not necessarily a bad sign as some, such as tulips, often shed all their skins without suffering any setback. Nevertheless I would avoid the more obviously balding specimens as this does suggest that they have been turned over and over by earlier customers and so might have been bruised. Bulbs are sold in marketable sizes, that is sizes that will in normal circumstances produce flowers; this is particularly the case with hyacinths. But there is no need to buy the expensive, specially prepared bulbs—hyacinths and some of the bunch-flowered narcissi—as these are treated to make them flower early indoors.

Make sure you plant your bulbs the right way up. This may seem a daft suggestion but I, who should have known better, once planted a hyacinth upside down in a pot and could not understand why the soil seemed to be rising up out of the pot instead of the expected leaf tips. When I turned the pot out I found a 4 inch spike underneath, perfectly formed but pure white like a head of chicory. Restored right way up it turned green and went on to produce a perfectly good flower head, but after that the bulb was spent because it had been unable to put down a proper root system. For long life in the garden bulbs need plenty of food because they are expected to last for more than one season and to go on to produce more plants via bulblets or seed. In a box it is asking too much to expect a bulb to perform year after year and you must be resigned to starting up with new ones every autumn. Use a good soil-based or soilless compost, never garden soil, and give some plant food such as Phostrogen when the buds are about to break. But bulbs that have one flower and are then spent are not as much in need of feeding as the annuals in the summer box that you must persuade to keep their flowers coming.

You may read that different bulbs have different soil requirements—hyacinths need particularly sandy soil and not much humus while tulips and daffodils will do in a bit of clay. But I have had considerable success with hyacinths in a peat-based

soilless compost, admittedly a nice open mix but hardly sand. Again the special requirements are for the long-term needs of the plant and the building up of colonies in the garden.

So what to do with all these bulbs you will have left when the box is finished? If you have a garden you have no problem. You simply heel them in, in a spare bit of the vegetable garden; that is, make a trench of the same depth as you first planted the bulb, lie the bulbs with their foliage in it and cover over with soil.

Remove flower heads so that energy is diverted back to the bulb rather than wasted in producing seed. During the summer the foliage will die back and you can lift the bulbs, dry them off and store them somewhere cool and dry until the time comes for planting them. You will probably lose some, and if you can plant the bulbs straight into their final positions you should have fewer losses. If you have no garden yourself then probably you possess friends who have and will be grateful for your cast-offs. If you haven't any gardening friends then you could easily acquire some, simply by accosting anyone you see working in his or her garden and asking if they would like them. Few would be so churlish as to refuse, and most would be delighted to accept. If accosting complete strangers and plying them with dead daffodils is not your style, then there's nothing for it but the dustbin. It may seem a shame, but how much did they actually cost? As much as a bottle of wine, or a bottle of gin, or a meal out? Fleeting pleasures, all.

SUMMER
High summer, when everything in the garden is blooming and burgeoning in competition, is the time when window boxes should be planted very boldly. Colours in the summer must be bright to compete with the sun or perhaps make up for the lack of it.

Red geraniums and dark blue trailing lobelia are something of a horticultural cliché but for effect against stone or stucco they can hardly be bettered. As a change from the red geranium—like 'Sprinter', which is massed outside Buckingham Palace every year—you can have 'Cherie', which has soft salmon pink flowers and deeply zoned leaves, or 'Ringo Salmon', which is almost orange, or 'Rose Marie', a really intense pink. If your house is built of brick avoid all the colours and choose white, either 'White Orbit' or 'Iceberg', which will look stunning. In fact when choosing geraniums the golden rule is to shop around because newer, more

exciting colours are introduced every season. When you have found a geranium in a shade you like, mass it for maximum effect.

French marigolds were once my *bête noire*, ugly, stiff and nasty smelling to boot. But now there are so many new colours, from lemon yellow to deep mahogany with bicolours in reds and golds, that I am beginning to change my mind. In window boxes they should be planted tightly to form a hedge of colour; try some of the carnation-flowered bicolours like 'Super Bonita', 'Joyful' or 'Red Cherry'. Insisting on particular varieties is not an affectation, like checking the vintage of a cheap supermarket wine. Because you are gardening in a very small space you have no room for mistakes or for effects that are merely tolerable. Pink may look all right with blue, but this particular salmon with bronze will look superb. By the same token, any orange with cerise will look frightful so do not be deflected from your search for good colour combinations. Specialist nurseries usually have the best selection of new varieties and are more sympathetic to your requests; market stalls are often cheaper but you can have any colour you like as long as it's red! For the best effects do your shopping via the seed catalogues and try raising your own plants on the indoor window sill.

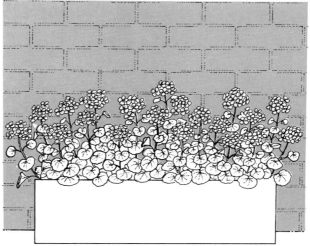

Against a red brick wall white geraniums look stunning.

Fuchsias usually look better in pots and tubs than in window boxes. They mix well with other summer annuals but look better if massed together. You can mix trailers and standards to give height and together they will give a good display for four months at least. Fuchsia names are rather endearing—'Ting-a-Ling', 'Tom Thumb', 'Mrs Popple'—and plants should be bought when flowering because the flowers are so difficult to describe. Pick off the tip shoots to make your bushes compact or take out all the side shoots if you want

taller standards. Fuchsias can be overwintered in a frost-free place.

There is no sadder sight than a petunia that has been rained on, unless it is one of the new weather-resistant varieties that don't crumple up like wet tissue after rain. So ask about weather tolerance when buying petunias and look for some of the newer colours: 'California Girl' is creamy yellow and 'Cherry Frost' and 'Blue Frost' have frilled white edges.

Impatiens is perhaps one of the best flowers for the summer box; it is happy in shade and doesn't need too much water. Although colours run from white through pale pink to scarlet and violet, the plants are often sold as mixed colour boxes. Unusually, with impatiens the mixing of shades is surprisingly effective.

Thunbergia alata, or black-eyed susan, comes in yellow, white and orange, usually with an attractive black eye. As climbers they grow well in hanging baskets; in boxes they trail prettily. 'Susie Mixed' or 'Alata Mixed' are the seeds to look for if you are raising your own plants; if you buy individual plants from a nursery they will probably come from one of these mixtures.

If you decide to buy plants rather than raising

them you will be restricted to those that the growers themselves choose to raise. These used always to be the more run-of-the-mill varieties but the trend today is towards newer and better colours and forms. So buy from the nursery that identifies its bedding plants. After all, bedding lobelia can mean anything from a wishy-washy blue so-called compact variety to a trailing dark blue with a white eye or a deep red trailer with a white eye; you can also have mixed cascade lobelias in all shades of blue, pink, mauve and white. Lobelia grows from minute seeds and makes equally tiny fragile seedlings so that by the time you buy them in boxes or strips both roots and shoots are inextricably tangled. Don't try to separate them, but break each strip up into half a dozen clumps and plant these firmly at the front of your containers. Never mind what you hear about giving plants room to grow; pack them in fairly close and be prepared to feed regularly to compensate for the crowded conditions. All bedding plants benefit from being dead-headed regularly so that their effort goes into producing more flowers rather than seed. Dead-heading lobelia is something of a Herculean task, so trim your clumps every couple of weeks once they have started blooming. If you do this carefully with kitchen scissors you will

keep the flowers coming without spoiling the shape of the plant.

Alyssum is always associated with lobelia—usually planted alternately along suburban front paths and all right, I suppose, if you like that sort of thing. Once available only in white, it can now be found in pinks and purples that have more charm. Ageratum, too, now comes in some really deep shades of lilac and blue, which makes it more appealing for the front of the box. Again, pack it in tightly.

Dianthus, the annual, is increasingly produced for window boxes and also for hanging baskets. Most varieties flower in flushes, three or four times during the season rather than continuously, so it is a good idea to plant a second basket three weeks later in the hope that when the flush in the first one is over you can quickly replace it with the second just coming into its best. I say hope, because that is what all gardeners live on; adverse weather or sheer perversity may still give you two baskets in flower at the same time. There are new varieties that are said to be continuous flowering so it is worth buying these if you can find them. Annual dianthus lack the scent of the old-fashioned garden pinks. For a scented tub or basket you could certainly plant some of these perennial pinks and enjoy their sweet

carnation perfume in the early part of the summer. By picking off dead blooms you can extend their flowering right through the summer although this will be at the expense of the plants' vigour. Perennial pinks are sold as small plants, so are more expensive than the annual bedding dianthus, but are still by no means costly. Discarding them at the end of the season would not be too extravagant a measure.

Another scented favourite is nicotiana, the tobacco plant. It has to be said that it is the old, white, tall, floppy one that smells most sweetly and as this usually opens its flowers at night it is hardly much of a subject for a show window box. Breeding has now produced self-supporting, day-blooming, early-flowering, coloured plants but has unfortunately been unable to preserve all the marvellous scent. No doubt they are working on it and in the meantime it is still a plant to be enjoyed. The dwarf varieties stand at 12 inches and look best *en masse*, or at the back of a box. In front, to pursue the cottage garden theme, I would put antirrhinums. These have now been extensively bred, both upwards to produce stately florists' specimens and downwards to make dwarf bedders with firm stems and neat habit. 'Tom Thumb' is one of the smallest

Hanging baskets should be packed tight with both flowering plants and compost. Sphagnum moss is used to line the basket and retain the compost; plants like lobelia or tiny cuttings of ivy or travescantia will grow happily through this lining. Baskets need watering at least once and sometimes three times a day in the summer, so hang them somewhere accessible.

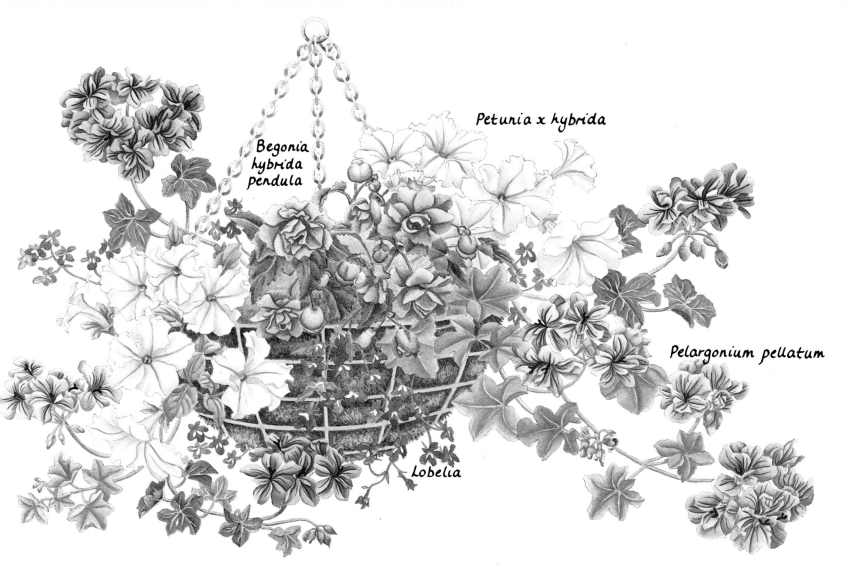

Begonia
hybrida
pendula

Petunia x hybrida

Pelargonium pellatum

Lobelia

at 8–12 inches, 'Pixie' and 'Little Darling' are a little taller but still suitable for box work and 'Minaret' hybrids are equally good and flower earlier. Since there is such a wide range of heights it is important to choose from the dwarf varieties. You pinch out the growing tips to make the bushes more compact and produce more, if smaller, spikes of flowers but you will not dwarf a really tall-growing variety this way, only stunt it.

Along the front of this cottage box I might put ageratum in soft powdery blue or mauve to offset all the pinks and reds. Or nasturtium to add to them. Try one of the 'Gleam' hybrids, which are climbers and semi-double, and if you cannot find plants buy seeds and bury them three-quarters of an inch deep in the box or basket. In three or four weeks you should have sizeable plants that, even if they are somewhat shy flowering, as they always seem to be for me, have nevertheless attractively shaped and marked leaves to trail across the front of the box. I have never seen godetia in a window box, nor tried it myself, but the new varieties seem tailor-made for the job. Dwarfs start at about 9 inches and those known as azalea-flowered really do merit the name. They like light compost and a sunny site and may be prone to various types of rot. You would know if

they had succumbed as this usually makes them collapse completely. In this case, whip them out quickly and plant something completely different; window boxes are not sanatoria and euthanasia is perfectly OK in the flower world.

Amaranthus or love-lies-bleeding is a favourite of mine though I can hardly imagine Yeats' 'fields of amaranth', so perhaps this is something different. The long pink tassels, which are very long lasting, are best seen in a hanging basket, or the plant, which is tallish at 2–3 feet, can be centred in a window box and allowed to flop forward, with a sturdier planting such as geranium or fibrous-rooted begonia coming through the middle.

Begonias fall into three distinct groups. The fibrous-rooted ones are evergreen and shrubby in appearance and are grown for their small pink or red flowers, although some have dark, almost black leaves that are very handsome. They are not as showy as the tuberous types but they are good-tempered, don't mind partial shade and flower almost endlessly if you pick off the dead blooms. Tuberous begonias have dramatic, sometimes scarcely real-looking blooms in red, white, pink and yellow. The non-stops really do flower continuously, producing large double flowers

in strong colours. The tubers are bought dry in early spring, planted hollow-side up in a box of nicely moist peat and kept indoors for warmth until growth starts. Once they have rooted—regrettably some may not, which is why you start them off this way first—move them into 4 inch pots, then finally into 6 inch ones. They are perhaps more trouble than other window box subjects but are well worth the effort. Slightly less effort, but equally rewarding in my book, are the pendulous varieties. These I start off as before then plant directly into small individual hanging baskets. One plant soon fills a small basket and the flowers, red, white or yellow, spill delightfully over the edge. A word about yellow begonias: they very often aren't. At least, whenever I plant a yellow one—and it is my favourite colour—I seem to get a red, which is disappointing. Then there are the rhizomatous begonias that are grown for their beautifully marked silvered and crimped leaves. The 'Caribbean' and 'Rex' hybrids look good in pots or baskets and can be brought indoors in the winter. I like to have two or three that I use to fill gaps in a box until other plants have come on; I leave them in their own pots and simply remove them, pot and all, as soon as they have done their duty.

At the end of summer tuberous begonias must be allowed to dry and the leaves to drop off. Then they can be stored in a frost-free place until spring but, understandably, the second year's flowers, even if you have fed the plant assiduously all the summer before, are never as proliferous. As a precaution, buy some fresh tubers each spring.

Verbena is an old-fashioned cottage garden plant that is making something of a comeback. It is really a perennial but is best treated as an annual; the new hybrids have dense heads of pink, white and purple flowers that still retain their scent. Take out the growing shoots to encourage bushiness and dead-head regularly. Verbena is usually sold in boxes of mixed colours and these mixtures are particularly attractive. It reaches a height of up to 10 inches.

Gazania is another perennial most commonly grown as an annual. G. × hybrida at 9 inches has dark green foliage with a grey underside; the daisy flowers are in the yellow, orange, bronze range though you can also have some deep pinks. They like full sun.

Marigolds—the nurseries call them calendula to distinguish them from French and African marigolds—have been bred to produce showier

and showier doubles in colours from vivid orange to almost lemon. Against a white-painted wall the subtle range of colours looks superb—most seeds and boxes are sold as mixed varieties and this mixing enhances their appearances. Marigolds need nipping out to keep them bushy and regular dead-heading, and that's about all.

What else can we plant in a summer box? The answer is: whatever you can find that meets the twin requirements of low growth and sturdy habit. Don't be put off by the man in the garden centre who won't recommend a plant for window boxes because he has never seen it grown that way. He is being, at least, honest but not very adventurous.

You may make a mistake or simply be sold a box of plants that does not perform as it is supposed to: nicotiana, perhaps, that come up 4 feet tall and plunge the sitting room into gloom, or nasturtiums that don't seem to have read the stuff on the seed packet about being a riot of flower all summer and produce nothing but a riot of leaves. If something goes wrong, throw it out and start again. Garden centres are full of quick-growing annuals from too early in the spring—late May is the earliest you should be planting many annuals and even then you can be taking a chance—until late summer. As the

season progresses, the plants in boxes become starved and it is only the desperate who will buy them. But as well as these boxes there are usually individually rooted plants, things like petunias, gazanias, dianthus and all the different marigolds. These can seem scandalously expensive to anyone who knows you can get hundreds from a small packet of seeds. But you are buying the grower's time as well as the seedling, so grit your teeth and buy a few to fill in gaps or replace earlier failures. Once settled into a new home, with more space to spread themselves plus regular feeding, these individually raised plants will usually romp away and quite take your mind off their original price.

It is axiomatic that, once you have bought plants for your box or boxes, you will have some left over. As a tender-hearted soul you will hate the thought of discarding perfectly healthy plants so the chances are you will hunt around for a pot or even another box in which to plant them. Then you have to buy a few more to fill it up, and have some more left over. . . . Summer is the time when you can indulge this proliferation of boxes and pots and it is surprising how many different containers can be pressed into service to take odd plants. Old catering-size tins or plastic ice-cream or fridge

boxes can have holes made in their bases and be used, perhaps only for one season, to provide extra splashes of colour around the house. Otherwise, use simple clay, not plastic, pots but be prepared to water them often.

If you have space at ground level you can extend your range of plants to take in some of the taller perennials. Stand their boxes against a wall and provide support for the growing stems and you can have even giants like hollyhocks or sunflowers to create interest at a higher level. Climbers can be grown in containers. Clematis, particularly, like to get their heads right up in the sun but need shade at their roots and I have seen them flourishing at first-floor window height when their roots were in a box in the deep shade of a basement area.

The many species clematis and the more familiar hybrids such as our old friend 'Nellie Moser' are worth a book in themselves, and indeed there are many that will give meticulous descriptions and full details on how to grow and prune each single variety.

You should always ask for advice on pruning when you buy a clematis. As a general rule you prune the species clematis only when you need to restrict their growth and this is simply a matter of

cutting out old and weak growth and shortening remaining shoots by up to two-thirds. The correct time for pruning summer and autumn flowering species is the following February or March; those that bloom in the spring or early summer you do immediately after flowering.

The magnificent hybrids, those that flower from the end of May until July, should be encouraged to make bushy growth low down rather than a bird's nest mass high up on thin spindly shoots. Usually all shoots are cut back to within 9 inches of the ground during the second spring after planting. After that it is a question of tidying up weak or dead wood and tying in young growth to trellis or training wires. The clematis that flower from July onwards can be encouraged to spread outwards rather than upwards by judicious tying in of shoots along horizontal wires; the flowers will grow upwards from these. Pruning the following spring means cutting back all this growth to a pair of plump buds near the base of these vertical shoots, and removing weak or dead wood. Clematis enthusiasts will tell you that there is hardly a month in the year when you cannot have a clematis in bloom. Certainly you can see *C. alpina*'s lilac bell flowers nodding away in April, while many of the large-flowered hybrids

start in May or June and keep going until October. Clematis like limey soil, though this is not essential; a good plan is to incorporate crushed mortar rubble or chalk in the compost in the pot. What *is* essential is shade for the roots, and usually this is best arranged by planting something low-growing just in front of your clematis.

Climbing roses will grow in tubs. Choose climbers rather than ramblers, as climbers grow more circumspectly and are less prone to mildew and other problems. The list is endless, but I would not like to be without 'Zephyrine Drouhin', despite her tendency to mildew, 'Handel', which is cream with rosy pink edges and has handsome bronze foliage, or 'Maigold', which is double yellow and beautifully scented. Some roses will flourish only on south walls while others are happy in a west or east aspect and others will even tolerate a north wall. Then there are those that are scented and those that are not, those that have one magnificent flowering and then call it a day and others that flower less prolifically but throughout the summer. Add to that those that retain at least some of their foliage through the winter and those that are beautiful but dreadfully prone to disease and you can see that it is very difficult to make a choice of even a dozen varieties,

A weeping standard rose in a half barrel container can stand in a small patio.

let alone a single one. Rather than choose on the spot in a crowded garden centre, do it at home with a good catalogue where you can agonize over scent and colour and habit until you have just the right rose. Don't be deflected once you have made up your mind, either. A friend in an absent moment bought 'Nevada' because she fell for its wonderful

Dahlias provide colour until the first sharp frosts and in sheltered positions can go on until October or November. Remove dead flowers regularly to keep blooms coming and stake the taller varieties. The dahlia box is best sited at ground level because even the lower growing varieties can reach three feet and more.

Decorative

Dahlias

Single flowered

Large semi~cactus

Anemone flowered

Miniature ball

Collerette

open flowers, forgetting that it is the very last rose for a tub since it can make prodigious growth and invariably gets leggy lower down. To say nothing of its wicked thorns—something to bear in mind in a restricted space. If you have room you can grow standard roses in tubs, using them as specimen 'trees', even weeping ones, in a tiny patio layout. Half barrels make ideal containers.

Roses should be given a good rich compost and regular applications of rose food. Pruning is usually a question of taking out dead and spindly growth and any shoots that are growing in the wrong direction or crossing one another, although it is best to seek advice on the correct treatment of any particular rose when you buy it. Remember, the grower always knows best.

Honeysuckle is an easygoing climber that can bring a country garden look to even the most suburban villa. Plant it in a good-sized tub and give it some trellis as a support; after that you must ruthlessly clip the long shoots to keep the bush furnished right down to the ground. Honeysuckle likes it a bit damp so will make growth even in a sunless spot, although the flowers will always head for the sun.

If you fancy a passion flower—the passion has religious rather than sexual connotations—you should be able to accommodate one on a sheltered sunny wall. It thrives best if the roots are restricted so is ideal in a tub; it will also need some wire trellis and will need tying in at first. Another climber that will give you flowers right up until the first frosts is *Cobea scandens.* It is a perennial but best treated as an annual, and as plants are not always available I find it best to raise new ones from seed every March on the indoor window sill. You soak the large seeds for two hours then plant them two or three to a Jiffy pot, taking out the weaker seedlings as growth begins. *C. scandens* can reach 15 feet in a season but restricted in a pot is more manageable. The flowers are huge violet bells that break from strange three-cornered buds; these are green at first and gradually turn purple. A well-grown plant is a remarkable sight and one that is bound to attract comment; the fact that it can be torn down and thrown out over winter is rather in its favour.

Lilies are another specialist subject about which whole books can be, and are, written. Surprisingly they are not all difficult to grow, and thrive in tubs. The bulbs appear in garden centres in the autumn and should be planted as soon as possible after purchase so that they don't dry out. The pots are then overwintered in a dark airy place, brought out when top growth appears in the spring and kept moist. The 'Enchantment' lilies are easy to grow and have dramatic orange-red flowers; so is the turk's-cap lily, *Lilium martagon*, which has beautifully recurved flowers in a rosy purple spotted with black. *L. regale* has white flowers with yellow-splashed centres and is fragrant. Buy lilies from their catalogue descriptions, choosing the hardy or easy varieties. Follow all the instructions, which can vary from variety to variety but are by no means difficult to understand, and you will be rewarded with some dramatic blooms.

As I have said, there is no end to the plants you can choose for a summer box. When you study catalogues, or seed packets, look for plants that have bold flowers, and pack them in well together. Feed them weekly with a liquid plant food and keep them well watered and you can hardly fail. If you do, then replacement is a simple matter. Summertime is when the living, and growing, is easy.

AUTUMN/WINTER

In the open garden autumn is a time of cutting down, tidying up and battening down the hatches against the onslaught of winter. In the more restricted garden on the window sill there is a little more scope for planting, to provide interest and perhaps colour for the grey days to follow. It is the greyness of the days, and hence the lack of light, rather than the cold that makes the late autumn and winter such a dead season as far as flowers are concerned.

For early autumn you must have dahlias. Their paint-box colours are quietened by the softer light of autumn and dahlia blooms laced with cobwebs and beaded with dew are, for me, a final confirmation that summer is truly over. For a window box you are limited to the dwarfer varieties but there is increasing choice even within these constraints. The ones to look for are the bedding dahlias, annuals grown from seed sown in February or March to produce both single and double blooms, and also, if you can cope with plants 20–24 inches tall, 'Collerette' types, singles with a central fringe of quilled petals. If you are buying bedding dahlias in a box the most you are likely to get by way of description is 'Coltness Hybrids'; this usually means gaily coloured single flowers, compact, but tending to run to 20–24 inches. Grown in the garden they need neither stopping nor disbudding, but in a box you can keep them within bounds by nipping out the top growth.

If you raise your own plants from seed, or can buy from a source where more attention is given to naming varieties, look for the latest in dwarf dahlias such as 'Dwarf Dahlfaced', which will produce flower buds at only 10–12 inches. These are singles, in every shade of pink, red and yellow. 'Rigoletto' at 12–14 inches includes doubles and semi-doubles, 'Redskin' of similar height is a good double mixture with deep red foliage and 'Dandy', 20–24 inches, is a single with a contrasting inner frill.

Dahlias require regular feeding, particularly as they need packing together tightly for best effect. Dead-head meticulously to keep the flowers coming and if your box is not too exposed they will probably go on for a week or two after the first frosts. Eventually, though, a frost will be sharp enough to bite and the tips will be blackened. There is no recovery from this condition, so throw everything out; you can start again with new plants in the spring.

Because dahlias usually come in mixed colours they look best as a single planting. But if you know you have single colours, or a range which runs from light to dark reds, you could include African marigolds in the planting. This would make a brilliantly fiery show, and again the African marigolds will get through a few early frosts if they are not too exposed.

Chrysanthemums are the other great glory of the autumn. For a box or tub there is less choice than there is among the taller garden varieties but still enough to make this a plant worth considering. It is a huge genus, with more than two hundred species of hardy and half hardy annuals, sub shrubs and herbaceous and greenhouse perennials. C. alpinum is one of the smallest at 6 inches with neat white flowers but, in July and August, a bit early for the autumn box. The annual varieties are hardy and easy to raise yourself from seed, but again start into flower in July although they can go on until September if you are lucky. Of the bedding varieties, 'Autumn Glory' makes well-shaped mounds from 12 to 20 inches in height and has small single flowers in the typical autumn pinks and bronzes, while 'Petit Point' has both single and double flowers.

Throughout the year, of course, you will see chrysanthemums offered as houseplants. These have been grown under controlled conditions to make them flower out of their natural season and also treated with a growth retardant to keep them low. If, like me, you think there is a time for everything

The winter box can have interest, with flowers, berries and leaves. Jasminum nudiflorum will flower as early as November or as late as April. Skimmia plants need to be planted in twos—one male and one female—to ensure a crop of berries. Most cotoneasters are evergreen, but c. horizontalis loses most of its leaves in winter leaving its berries elegantly displayed on near-bare branches.

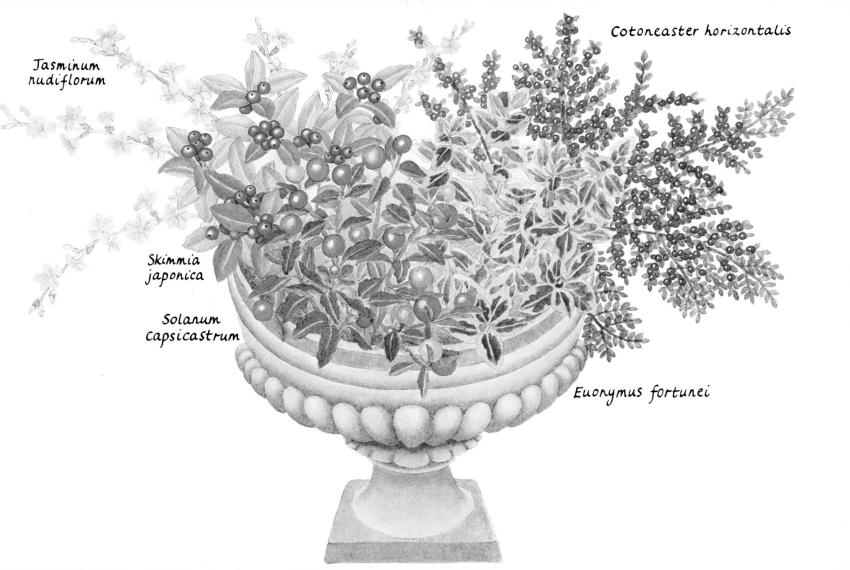

Cotoneaster horizontalis

Jasminum
nudiflorum

Skimmia
japonica

Solanum
capsicastrum

Euonymus fortunei

 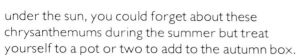
under the sun, you could forget about these chrysanthemums during the summer but treat yourself to a pot or two to add to the autumn box.

Chrysanthemum parthenium is a native of Great Britain and is regarded as a weed in many gardens. It has bright green aromatic leaves and white flowers, either double or single, freely produced from July to September. 'Aureum', 18 inches, has single white flowers, 'Golden Ball' at 10 inches has yellow flowers and 'Snow Dwarf' at 12 inches has ivory white pompoms. Any of these do well in a box and can be valued as much for their vivid light green leaves as for their flowers. *C. parthenium* is, of course, feverfew, which is said to help migraine sufferers if they are strong-stomached enough to eat two of the bitter leaves every day for six months.

Cobea scandens is another late flowerer—better for a large tub than a small box—and will go on flowering late into the year if it is protected from frost. Whether or not your box is protected from frost is something you can only find out the hard way. But, as any central heating expert will tell you, heat is lost through walls and windows at a rate of knots and this should benefit any plants grown just outside.

For a winter display it is form rather than colour that will provide interest. The plants grown in the all-season box, ivy, hebe, cotoneaster, for instance, will provide an interesting framework, and colour too if the cotoneaster produces good berries. Laurel, *Aucuba japonica* 'Maculata' particularly, is not to be despised and indeed is coming back into favour for winter boxes and containers. You must make sure you buy one male to three female plants to ensure a crop of berries but even if you haven't room for four plants you can still enjoy the yellow marked leaves. For fragrant, if small, white flowers in December to March there is *Sarcococca humilis*; glossy dark red berries make this an attractive plant over a long period.

Heathers are a subject in themselves (*qv*) and are now often used in boxes and containers, particularly in conjunction with dwarf and miniature conifers. For winter colour make sure you choose from *Erica carnea*, with white or pink flowers from November through till May and leaves which range from light green to dull yellow and bronze. Varieties include 'Praecox Rubra', with deep pink flowers from December, 'Cecilia M Beale', which has white flowers from December, and 'Loughrigg', with dark leaves which turn bronze and pinkish purple flowers in February.

In some of the splendidly maintained City of London boxes you may see the bright red berries of solanum, the winter cherry. These are more usually grown as indoor plants and are sold widely during the pre-Christmas rush. All through the festivities they struggle nobly with the dry heat indoors but are soon reduced to leafless branches and a few brave berries. They are usually thrown out along with the decorations on Twelfth Night. Outside in a window box they should last longer, providing it is not frightfully cold, because they appreciate the moister air. But they should be regarded as only a short-term investment since sooner or later they will succumb to the cold. Sink them, still in their pots, in a winter box to provide a little temporary cheer.

And that seems to sum up the autumn/winter box. Temporary cheer, slotted into a framework of green, using plants that you know will succumb sooner rather than later. But by Christmas time the first sprouted daffodils are being sold for indoor use, and these can be encouraged into growth inside then popped into place in the winter box for a few early flowers. A bit of a shock to the plants, poor things, but shock, and the possibility of an early demise, is often what stimulates them into bigger and better flowers.

THE INSTANT BOX

Window boxes are often impulse acquisitions. You are halted in your tracks by a wonderful display of bedding plants and there is nothing for it, you must have some. No garden? Never mind, there is room for a few window boxes. . . .

Such impulses can be the beginning of a long and enjoyable acquaintanceship with window box gardening. They can also be the reason behind the starved and unhappy specimens you sometimes see as the summer draws on, the unwanted kittens of window box gardening that you cannot give away and that certainly don't seem destined for a death by drowning. If your first boxes are impulse buys, or if you know only too well that you are one of those people whose early enthusiasm is liable to wane, then hold your horses for a moment and plan.

You must have some of those gorgeous polyanthus, primulas, petunias? You suddenly can't live without geraniums red and lobelia blue along the window sill? Then fill your box not with compost but with aggregate—washed gravel or, if you are concerned about the weight, and gravel *is* heavy, with those lightweight brown pebbles commonly sold for use on greenhouse staging. As these are not cheap you can economize by using a deeper-than-usual layer of broken brick first. As you fill with your finer medium, gravel or pebbles, settle into position as many 3½ inch pots as the box will take. Push them up close and fill up any final gaps with smaller pots so that you can accommodate the maximum number of plants. Your choice should be from among those ready-potted specimens, rather than from the boxes or strips in which bedding plants are usually sold. These potted plants are more expensive, of course, but they will be settled in and in bloom. Choose plants that have a good supply of buds to follow, so as to get the maximum out of your plant before you consign it to the rubbish bin and replace it with something else just coming into flower.

Your instant no-fuss box could begin in spring with polyanthus, or even earlier with pansies. These should bloom merrily until the first summer bedding plants appear. Here you have a decided advantage over the open gardener, because the first bedding plants appear in garden centres and on market stalls in time for Whitsun, the weekend when even the most reluctant gardener is prodded into action. Since Whitsun is a movable feast this can be any time between mid-April and early June, and the earlier date can be much too early for planting out in the open garden. Quite sharp frosts can occur until well into May, but these are unlikely to affect plants grown close to the house in window boxes. Small consolation perhaps, but if your massive heating bills are a result of too much heat pouring out through walls and windows, you are at least keeping your window boxes warm!

The first plants to choose as replacements for your polyanthus and pansies could be antirrhinums; these are now available as quite dwarf specimens— 'Humming Bird' is a very early flowering variety in a good range of bright colours and only 8 inches tall; 'Pixie' is a good mixture that reaches 10 inches; and 'Little Gem' is a real dwarf at 4–6 inches. If you cannot find these individual varieties potted singly, the names at least will serve as a guide when you ask for help with your selection.

Begonia rex and caladium are most often grown as greenhouse or indoor plants and for their dramatic leaf colouring. You could plant them up in an attractive container and set them outside if the weather is gentle, but a better site would be a window sill or porch.

Begonia rex

Caladium

Marigolds—calendula nowadays—are another toughie that can come into flower early and are reasonably low growing. *Begonia semperflorens*, the fibrous-rooted begonias, make a good long-lasting show; impatiens are easy, low growing and now come in double as well as single varieties. Look for the doubles, which have flowers like miniature roses. Calceolarias are not everybody's favourite—close up they look rather like something that should be removed without further delay by a competent surgeon—but their effect, *en masse* and from a distance, is very colourful. They will even tolerate a shady position, which is not common in brightly coloured plants. African marigolds come in shades from clear lemon right through to the more usual oranges to a lovely rich mahogany. There are single and double varieties and some are attractively bicoloured. The more interesting African and French marigolds are often sold potted singly and all you have to beware of are the larger types, usually of African marigolds, that can get as high as 3 feet. Both African and French marigolds are very erect of habit, so good for a window box; the feathery leaves are attractive too.

Petunias have now become much more weather resistant. In any case, in a window box there is usually sufficient protection for them not to crumple up like damp tissues after a shower of rain. Garden centres usually offer the more elegant new varieties potted singly and you should be able to find frilled and bicoloured types to make a good display.

It has to be admitted that most bedding plants would prefer not to be kept in the restricted space of a flower-pot. In compensation they will need very regular watering and feeding. Keeping a permanent supply of water at the base of the gravel-filled instant box is not as good an idea as it might at first seem. The plants would certainly benefit from the damp micro-climate that would develop as the water vapour was drawn up around them but there is a danger that this water would become dank, slimy and even smelly as the season wore on. The aggregate may, indeed should, be kept moist but the water should be allowed to dry out from time to time. To save having to root around in it to see how much water is at the bottom you can insert a piece of narrow tubing in one corner of the box. Anything will do; a piece of plastic piping of the sort sold for plumbing is probably best, but you can improvise with anything you have at hand that will allow you to insert a 'dip-stick' from time to time to check the water level. Allow the water to dry out for a few days at a time, but never the compost in the pots. Of course this only applies if your boxes are of plastic or some other inorganic material; wooden boxes would rot if water stood in them for long periods. Pick over your plants regularly and remove dead leaves and flowers to encourage buds to open and to prolong the attractive life of the plant.

Care and feeding notwithstanding, instant boxes need regular replenishment. Primroses might go on for six to eight weeks before the last buds fade and pansies could go on even longer. *Begonia semperflorens* and impatiens would certainly keep going all summer and could even be cut back and allowed to come again for a winter flowering indoors. But this is not the point of an instant box. An instant box is an excuse to fall for irresistible impulses or an opportunity to masquerade as a real gardening buff when all you have actually done is to swap one faded shop-bought plant for a bright new one. Certainly it allows you to smarten up the house painlessly if a visitation of in-laws is imminent or if you have suddenly decided to sell the place and want to make a good first impression.

To 'plant' your new acquisitions simply tap them out of their pots and drop them straight into the pots you have already positioned. Water them well first, and they should drop out easily; if not, tap them smartly and try again. Avoid tugging at the top of the plant or disturbing the roots because this will set the plant back and what you are trying to achieve is instant effect. If the roots are growing strongly through the holes in the bottom of the pot you should not have bought it in the first place; cut through the pot with strong scissors rather than destroy the roots in this case.

If throwing out everything and beginning again every six weeks or so becomes too expensive then you can drop down a gear and simply top up. Put in a few of those fibrous-rooted begonias that will keep going as long as you dead-head them and simply add the occasional individual plant. Or give your indoor plants a summer break by sinking them into the aggregate. They will provide greenery, while themselves benefiting enormously from a spell in the fresh air and sun. Splashes of colour can be introduced as and when you spot them. For bargains, look in markets, especially those in the centre of towns or cities. Here the emphasis is on quick turnover as no one wants to cart unsold plants home again; you may not see the most exciting new varieties but you should spot some cheap and cheerful additions to the instant box.

Boxes from Inside the House

THE ALPINE BOX

Walk around any garden centre on a Sunday morning in spring and you will be sure to see people cooing over the alpine section. Oh! what a lovely flower, they say, so tiny and delicate, and into the basket it goes. Back home there's often neither rock garden nor dry wall, so they pop it hopefully into one of those empty spaces of which the garden seems so full at the beginning of the season. There it will flower bravely for a week or two, unregarded by any but the odd passing cat, until a forgotten clump of hostas emerges to nudge it into an early grave.

Alpines are an impulse buy. But as a window box gardener you are uniquely able to fall for these horticultural equivalents of chocolate bars at the checkout because you are going to grow them properly, in the gritty soil they love. You are going to water them well in spring, give them plenty of light and air. Most important of all, you are going to enjoy them in all their seasons because on a window sill they are so much closer to eye level.

Traditionally alpines are grown in rocky surroundings, in a rock garden or in a wall or a table bed. Tell the specialist rock gardener that you are planting yours in a plastic window box and he will probably roll his eyes in horror. So don't tell him. Plastic will be fine, because from where you will look down on your display all you will see is the plastic rim. Even this will soon disappear as plants expand and trailers start to trail. The advantage of a plastic box is its lightness, which helps to compensate for the extra weight of the stone that is part of the display. Equally light are some of the mock stone containers that are available, fibreglass or plastic imitations that are not to everyone's taste but that can look very effective in an alpine display.

Alpines will grow happily in containers fitted with sharply draining, gritty soil. Nicely shaped matching rock is decorative, and authentic, and also provides the cool anchorage which alpine plants need. Sedums provide interest throughout the year with their sharply-tipped fleshy leaves, then surprise us with tall, stately blooms in summer.

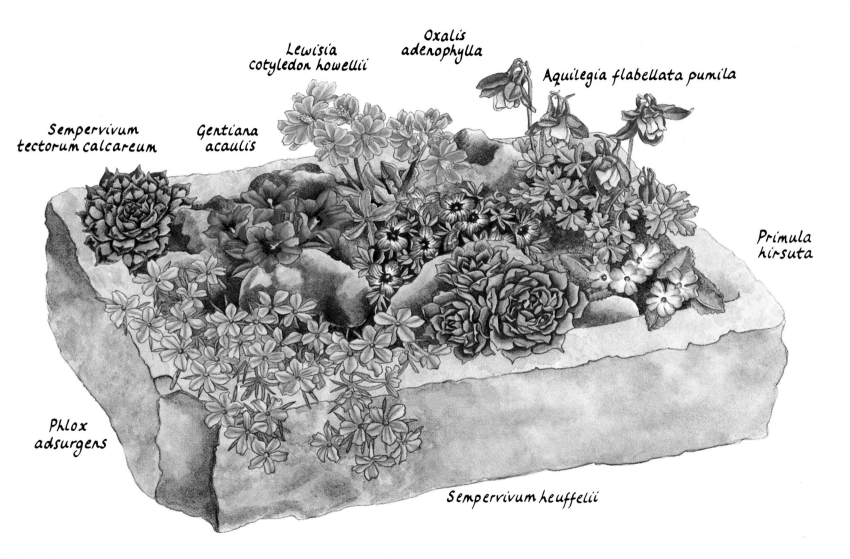

Lewisia
cotyledon howellii

Oxalis
adenophylla

Aquilegia flabellata pumila

Sempervivum
tectorum calcareum

Gentiana
acaulis

Primula
hirsuta

Phlox
adsurgens

Sempervivum heuffelii

Alternatively choose wood, or any other kind you like. White is the best colour, or black or grey, and your box will need a drip-tray because watering will be frequent.

The alpine box should be filled with John Innes compost no. 3 opened up further with fine stone chips, sand or grit, all usually available from garden centres. You will also need coarse peat to cover a drainage layer of broken flower-pots and small pieces of brick; since these aren't too easy to find in cities you should talk nicely to your local garden centre and get in a good supply. You can at the same time organize your rocks, choosing from the smaller pieces that break off rockery stone. These are usually sold quite cheaply, by the pound.

Don't let yourself be hurried when you choose your rocks because these will be permanent features of your mini-alp. Sort out some with attractive striations and shapes that can be grouped together to simulate a natural outcrop of rock. Choose a few larger pieces rather than a lot of small ones, which can look like so many almonds on the top of a trifle, and stick to one type of rock throughout. Mixes of stone and sandstone and that nice piece you found on the beach will look awkward and unnatural. Buy rather more than you

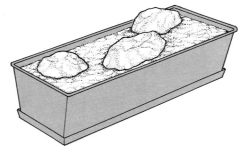

Use well-matched rock for the best effect in an alpine box.

think you will need to give yourself plenty of scope. When you have all your filling together, soil, grit, drainage material and rocks, you can make a start. Check that drainage holes are clear and punch out more if necessary, then put in a good layer of broken pots and bricks—about 2 inches in an 8 inch box. On top goes a layer of coarse peat, just enough to keep fine soil from washing through and clogging the drainage holes. Then in goes the compost, well mixed with the grit, sand or chips in the proportion of two parts compost to one part grit. Do this on newspaper on the floor if necessary, to ensure a good mix. Fill the box right to the top as the mix will soon settle.

Bed rocks firmly in the ground but not too deeply. Plant roots will then be able to find a cool anchorage beneath them. And do get your layout right, with

strata uniformly lined up. If it doesn't look natural now it won't look any better once it's planted, I promise you. If you can't get it to your satisfaction buy a few more rocks or settle for one large rock only. The artlessly natural look does take a bit of time to achieve. Water the box well, check that water can escape through the drainage holes and leave it all to settle for a couple of days.

In the meantime you can be choosing plants. Your mini-alp will need a tree so the first purchase should be a dwarf conifer, with the emphasis on the word dwarf. Since conifers can reach prodigious heights in the wild, dwarf to a nurseryman sometimes means only 3 or 4 feet high, but what you want is one that is perhaps 6 inches tall now and that will take five years to double its height. Some garden centres display these mini conifers separately or label them suitable for sinks and troughs. Don't be tempted to buy anything but a really dwarf variety or your alpine landscape will soon get decidedly out of scale.

The conifers you are most likely to find will include *Juniperus communis* 'Compressa', sometimes called the noah's ark juniper, and this is one of the best for a small display. Its shape is like a candle flame and its growth is dense and a pleasant blueish green; it is also one of the slowest growing conifers, taking many years to reach even 12 inches in height. Then there is the so-called tennis ball cypress, *Chaemaecyparis obtusa nana* 'Tetragona Minima', which is a terrible mouthful for a nice dark mound of a tree with tight, fan-like growth. *C. obtusa nana* 'Aurea' has more open growth in a brighter green edged with yellow. The Norway spruce has produced a few small varieties of which *Picea abies humilis* has a low annual growth rate and a compact roundish shape with dark shiny leaves. Thujas, the arbor-vitae, also have a few dwarf forms such as *Thuja orientalis minima glauca*, bun-shaped with fine needles. Taxus, the yew, has a slow-growing dwarf form, *Taxus baccata pygmaea*, with oval grey-green leaves.

Because Latin names for plants are constantly changing and because distribution of the less common ones is patchy, your garden centre may make other suggestions. If you think they are on the level, be guided by their advice. One way to check for yourself a tree's annual growth rate is to buy in April or May. Then the new growth will be a tender green, standing out well against the older, darker foliage; from this you can easily work out how soon your tree will double in height. Plant your tree to one side of a rock to give the layout a sense of scale,

and preferably at one end of the box rather than in the middle.

Your choice of plants should be restricted to those whose flowers stand no more than 4 inches tall so it is a good idea to buy them in bud or flower. A plant's eventual spread is not so important as this can be kept in check by removing too vigorous side growth or, more radically, by dividing the plant up after flowering and replanting only a small piece. To keep things in proportion you will need some low-growing plants that form neat clumps. *Armeria juniperifolia*, a sea thrift from Spain sometimes sold as *A. caespitosa*, is a good example. But whereas 'Bevan's Variety' makes a tidy 2½ inch tussock of narrow leaves and pink almost stemless flowers, *A. maritima*, runs in its 'Bloodstone' variety to dark red flowers 8–10 inches high. So it is important to get your varieties right and to look out for wrongly replaced labels on garden centre plants.

Other clump-forming plants of suitable height include varieties of dianthus or pink, potentilla, thyme, saxifrage, lewisia and many more.

To clothe the sides of your box you will need some trailers. Miniature phlox are often thought too rampant for container growing but a good hard clip with scissors after flowering usually keeps them tidy.

Polygonum is another plant that gets out of hand in the garden but my *Polygonum vacciniifolium* trails nicely over a stone sink edge and sends up spikes of rosy flowers sometimes as late as Christmas. Then there are the sedums. The stonecrop *Sedum acre* is undoubtedly a bit of a spreader, though its golden form is less so and unwanted bits are easily tweaked out of light soil. Other sedums, with shiny rosy leaves and red knobbly stems, will creep over edges and across rocks.

Plants are usually bought for the colour of their flowers but in an alpine box foliage colour can create interest all through the year. Grey-leaved plants, dianthus, the woolly thyme *Thymus lanuginosus*, a saxifrage such as *Saxifraga burserana*, will look delightful in combination with the blue-green of *Juniperus communis* 'Compressa', while for colour when not much else is happening there is *Sedum spathulifolium* with grey-green spoon-shaped leaves flushed with red or purple.

Between the low clumps and the taller trees you will need some mini shrubs. *Helichrysum selago* makes a rounded bush of erect stems covered with tiny scale-like grey leaves; this will eventually reach about 9 inches in height. The branches of *H. corralloides* are so overlapped with leaves that it

Wrap the roots of tiny plants in
damp tissue for protection—
then tuck them into the smallest
crevice.

does look very like branched coral and this is a
striking if somewhat tender plant. Just how much to
be inhibited by labels like tender or short-lived is a
matter of personal choice. Obviously it is silly to
spend money on really tender things unless you are
prepared to bring them indoors somewhere very
light and airy or be resigned to losing them when
the weather turns nasty. But if you are very taken
with a plant and it is just on the borderline of
hardiness, it is worth taking a chance. Alpines can
usually cope with cold; it is damp and soggy cold
weather that kills them off. If you keep your box
drier in winter and if it isn't plagued by heavy rain or
drips from guttering, you may be surprised at how
well plants overwinter.

More important when choosing plants is to stick
to lime-lovers or a mixture of these and others that
are tolerant of most soils. This includes the majority
of the easier alpines and all of those mentioned so far.

The plants you buy will be in pots and to fit them
into position you will probably need to remove
some of the soil. Tease this off the roots gently and
remove any bits of drainage crock. Make your
planting hole deep enough to take the roots without
bending them back on themselves and trim any very
long ones judiciously with nail scissors.

The popular plants you find in garden centres are
unlikely to have very long roots and may well be
newly rooted cuttings being sold a little too soon. If
this is the case, make the best of it by wrapping the
small roots gently in a scrap of damp tissue for
protection, then tucking them into a small crevice.
The tissue will soon rot and if the roots can get away
under a rock you will have managed to use an
otherwise unfillable corner.

When the final plant is in position—if such a thing
exists once you have caught the alpine bug—give
everything a good going-over with a fine mist spray
to clean soil off leaves and rocks. Then gently
distribute a top dressing of small chips. Limestone
chips and gravel can usually be bought by the bag
from builders' merchants if you can't get them at the
garden centre; another possible source is a pet shop

selling aquariums. Small chips look better than large ones and a mix of limestone and gravel is to my mind a more sympathetic colour than all limestone, which is very grey. A lot will depend on the colour of your rock and usually the best effect comes from crushing up spare rock with a hefty hammer and sprinkling the pieces around. Once your alpine box is planted it will need almost daily watering on dry spring and summer days. Don't overwater or rot will set in; the ideal condition is a soil that feels damp but not soggy. Correct any tendency for water to stand in puddles by adding more grit. It is difficult to understand that plants can revel in something as gritty as grit, but alpines certainly do. You should not need to feed plants in their first year. The soil in which they are forced on for quick sale is often a bit rich and this, combined with the nutrients already in the JI compost, should be more than enough. Later, as you take out old plants and introduce new ones, you will add more rich soil. If you do feel the need to feed, water in a Phostrogen solution during the active period and after flowering. But overfeeding is a mistake, as alpines like to struggle a bit for their existence. Never feed in winter and reduce watering at this time.

Serious gardeners always label plants but this

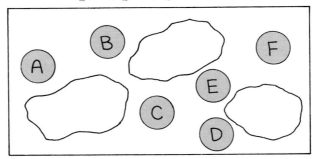

A	CAMPANULA CARPATICA
B	DIANTHUS DELTOIDES
C	HELIATHEMUM NUMMULARIUM
D	AUBRETIA DELTOIDEA
E	SAXIFRAGA MOSCHATA
F	DIANTHUS CAESIUS

Identify your alpines on a separate planting plan, as plant labels spoil the decorative effect and are also often misplaced.

spoils the effect in a window box, where labels tend to look like discarded lollipop sticks. A planting plan showing every plant identified with its proper Latin names is a better idea, especially when you discover how long and unmemorable some of these names can be.

HOW TO MAKE A SINK GARDEN USING HYPERTUFA

Old stone sinks make the perfect setting for rock plants but are largely unobtainable today. Shallow Victorian stoneware sinks can sometimes be found, especially in unconverted properties, but the most easily acquired sink is the 1930s style glazed porcelain type. With a coat of hypertufa this can be transformed into a very creditable version of the original stone sink.

First wash the sink with a strong soda solution to clean off any dirt and grease, then score the outside with a sharp edge to roughen the glaze. Make up a dry mix of fine grade peat moss, cement and sharp sand in equal quantities, add water and stir until the peat takes up water and the mixture feels crumbly and not too wet. Paint the outside of the sink— propped up temporarily on bricks—over the edges, down inside for 3 or 4 inches and a little way underneath with a bonding liquid such as Unibond. Leave for ten minutes or so until it feels tacky, then take up handfuls of mix and slap them gently against the sides. Press and spread as you go to make a dense and slightly uneven layer. Go down well inside the sink so that no white will show when it is

filled and keep the bottom edge neat; jagged edges could get knocked off accidentally later. The covering builds up surprisingly easily and stays workable long enough for you to tidy up edges and square off the rim to achieve an authentic outline. Add more water if it feels too dry but not too much or the finish will crack as it dries. Leave the sink, lightly covered in damp weather but otherwise untouched, until it is really dry. After about a week it can be propped up on bricks in its final position. The water outlet should be covered on the inside with perforated zinc if possible—if not, an old nylon tea-strainer will do. This is to prevent insects from creeping in. Don't plug the hole completely as it is needed for drainage; for this reason the sink should be tilted slightly in the direction of the outlet. Fill the sink as for a window box, substituting a layer of upturned turf, if such a thing can be found, for the layer of peat. This makes a better barrier and reduces the cost of using all compost. But don't use all garden soil as it is bound to be full of weeds and will compact badly after watering.

The hypertufa mix dries to a stone colour and the effect can be enhanced by painting with water in which rice has been boiled to encourage the growth of moss and lichens.

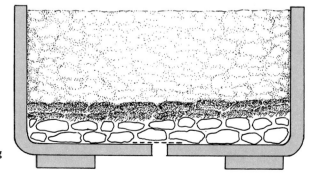

Sinks must be well drained. Leave the drainage hole unstopped and use a layer of perforated zinc or plastic netting to keep out ants and woodlice.

83

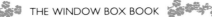

THE CACTUS BOX

Cacti and succulents are not hardy enough to stay out of doors throughout the year but will always benefit from spending the warmer months out in the air and sun. They are perhaps the most misunderstood of all plants. Somehow the myth has grown up that they can live indefinitely without water and this is what many of them must, perforce, do, usually in some ill-lit corner of the house where nothing else would be expected to survive. But water them correctly—not at all between December and March, then one good soaking every three or four weeks until June, followed by weekly watering and even daily spraying—and you will see them in a new light. Neglected specimens from indoors or, even better, well-cared-for plants from a nursery can go out on the window sill in late May or early June. Again, fill the box with gravel, settle in a nice rockscape and plunge in specimens still in their pots. Decorate the scene with finely crushed gravel.

The choice and variety of cacti is enormous. Opuntia are the ones that make round pads like rabbits' ears and these can be anything from a few inches to many feet tall. *O. brasiliensis* has a tree-like growth and very pronounced spines while *O. microdasys* is covered with tufts of yellow bristles. *O. rufida* has more oval-shaped pads and reddish brown bristles while *O. cylindrica* is columnar in shape and more like the cactus you see in all the best Westerns. The round cushion-like types are mammillaria; these have hooked spines and, if you are lucky, white or pink daisy-like flowers. *Echinocactus grusonii* has wickedly sharp yellow spines and for this reason is sometimes called mother-in-law's chair; *Chamaecereus silvestrii,* the peanut cactus, forms dense bunches of peanut-like pads and has red flowers, while *Cephalocereus senilis,* the old man cactus, is columnar and covered with long silvery hairs like an old man's beard.

These five types alone offer a range of different and unusual shapes so that even if you are not rewarded with flowers you could group them in a desert landscape and get a most interesting effect. But a visit to a garden centre with a well-stocked cactus section or, better still, to a cactus specialist will reveal dozens, maybe hundreds more.

As with most things horticultural you have to pay

Cacti are widely misunderstood. They need plenty of light and regular watering in summer, but little or no attention in winter. Their flowers are spectacular, but even when not in flower the shape and prickles have a charm of their own.

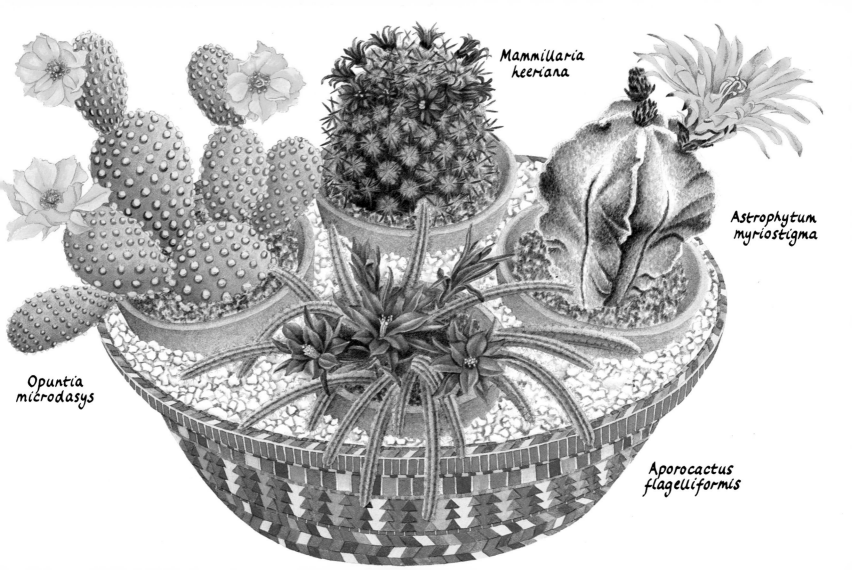

Mammillaria heeriana

Astrophytum myriostigma

Opuntia microdasys

Aporocactus flagelliformis

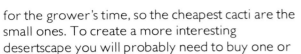

for the grower's time, so the cheapest cacti are the small ones. To create a more interesting desertscape you will probably need to buy one or two larger, more expensive specimens, so it is as well to know how to select good ones.

First and foremost a cactus should be well-rooted, so check that it does not rock in, or almost out of, its pot. Many cacti root very shallowly, but there is no reason why roots should not be firm. The trouble is that in transportation many get uprooted, and since they don't immediately wilt as a less adaptable plant would, they are offered for sale in this undesirable condition.

A well-grown cactus should have no brown patches on its pads, as these are usually signs of insect damage, frost damage or overwatering in winter. On the other hand, a large and therefore mature specimen will probably collect a few scars along the way, so it is a question of deciding (a) whether you think the seller is on the level and (b) whether the scars are too disfiguring. Buds and flowers are often a good sign as these indicate that the plant has been well treated, but absence of flowers may simply be because the type is immature, or shy flowering.

Alongside the cacti you will also see succulents,

which are plants with fleshy leaves or stems that store water. Cacti are a distinct group of succulents, most of which are leafless and on most of which can be found spines, needles, hairs, barbs, hooks and other hazards. Handling them with gloves, tweezers or very, very carefully is the only answer. If you are bitten, never try to remove spines with your teeth or you may end up with spines in your lips and tongue as well.

Succulents are easier to handle, though some of the agaves have sharply toothed leaves. Crassulas make good tree-like subjects for a desertscape. *C. argentea*, the jade plant or money tree, could be combined with an aloe such as *A. humilis*, the hedgehog aloe, which is predictably very spiny, or with one of the echeverias, which make nice rosettes of fleshy, sharply tipped leaves. Sempervivums are not dissimilar in shape and *S. arachnoideum*, the cobweb houseleek, is covered with a netting of fine cobwebby hairs. Among the sedums you can have *S. morganianum*, which grows down like a donkey's tail, or *S. rubrotinctum*, the jelly bean plant, which looks just like that. *Senecio rowleyanus* is the string of beads plant, which grows tiny strings of green beadlike leaves. Lithops are pebble-like plants that are fascinating in themselves

and very much more so when sporting their large daisy flowers.

To make a good desertscape you will need a variety of shapes and sizes in cacti and succulents and a few pieces of matching and fairly dramatic looking rock. Rocks should be jagged rather than softly rounded; think of your average Western and you will get the picture. Sand is obviously the right topping for a desertscape, and if you can get hold of different coloured sands and ones that are compatible with the colour of your rocks you can have a lot of fun laying them out.

The plants themselves will need more than sand in which to grow. If your cacti and succulents remain in their pots these will come to no harm if lightly covered with sand. Feeding is rarely necessary as most plants will need to be repotted in spring after their winter indoors.

Both cacti and succulents are easy to root from cuttings and these can be used to provide the variation in size that a good landscape needs. Whole sections of pads, or perhaps a slice of a pad, can be taken any time in summer when the plant is active. Cut edges should be left to dry out for a few days, or even weeks, before planting in a very sandy compost. Rooting can take place in a week or two or after as long as several months, so don't throw out any unless they look really shrivelled or rotten.

If you want cuttings to take while still contributing to the overall scene you will have to offer them a better medium than pure sand or gravel. Perhaps the best method would be to sink thumb pots of good cactus mix (sold as such by nurseries and garden centres) into the base gravel and let the cuttings root through the sand into this richer mix. When the time comes to break up the landscape and bring the plants indoors for the winter, you can lift the rooted cuttings out without disturbance and grow them on for another day.

Sedums and sempervivums, however, are often hardy and grow outdoors all the year through in dry walls and rock gardens. If you incorporate these in your plan you can leave them *in situ* all winter, simply removing the more delicate specimens for overwintering indoors. In this case, fill the box with gravel to a rather lower level and provide a top couple of inches of good sharp-draining soil. You can still plunge pots into this and finish them off with sand, and the sedums and sempervivums will have a little nourishment in their year-round stations.

Once you get bitten by the cactus bug, and have become immune, as you eventually do, to the cactus

spine, you will find seed a highly satisfactory way of acquiring new stock. Use the special cactus seed compost sold by garden centres and cover this with a layer of fine sharp sand. Sprinkle the seeds lightly and water them in with a fine mist spray so as not to disturb them. Warm water (at least 68 °F) helps germination and the young plants, which don't look a bit like fully-grown cacti, should stay in their original seed tray for twelve to eighteen months before being transplanted. This is mainly because they object to being disturbed when young but it also allows the slower types to germinate.

THE BONSAI BOX

Only so much as whisper to a serious bonsai enthusiast that you are thinking of growing bonsai trees in a window box and you will probably be greeted by howls of protest. But if you are unfamiliar with the art of growing bonsai—and it is an art, and no less surrounded with ritual than the Japanese tea ceremony itself—you could make a very creditable start with a few small subjects on your window ledge. These need not be expensive but they will give you the opportunity to practise some of the bonsai techniques and to see whether the conditions your window ledge offers are right for these rather demanding subjects. If they are, and you have been bitten by the bug, you will feel more confident about treating yourself to more mature, and more expensive, trees. If the enthusiasm wanes, or your lifestyle does not admit of the frequent watering necessary in very hot weather, you will still have had the pleasure of creating a tiny forest of seedlings, or a mini landscape of rocks and trees.

Mature trees are sometimes offered for sale in shops and garden centres but unless these have staff who know how to care for them properly I would hesitate to buy. Go instead to a bonsai specialist, and here you will be able to buy mature trees and also small seedlings of beech, silver birch, larch, hawthorn or maple, or perhaps rooted cuttings of some of the smaller-leaved garden shrubs such as

Bonsai means a tree in a tray and this is how the true bonsai expert likes to display a specimen. The pot is Japanese stoneware which is frost resistant. Bonsai can be brought indoors for enjoyment from time to time, but should spend most of the year out of doors in a spot which is sheltered from the wind.

Malas baccata
mandshumca

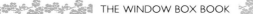

cotoneaster or pyracantha. These, although not established bonsai, will have been prepared for bonsai growing.

Seedlings and cuttings are sold still growing in small plastic pots and the first step is usually to lift them from these and prune the roots, to fit them into smaller pots. This is quite different from the normal repotting treatment, but with bonsai the aim is to keep the subject small, not help it grow bigger. If you are buying from a specialist you should ask when the seedling was last root-pruned and when it should be done again. With luck, if pruning is necessary he will do it for you while you watch so that you will know how to do it for yourself when the time comes, usually in the dormant season between November and March and ideally just before new growth appears in February or March. The procedure is to shake away the soil, tease out the roots that will have been growing around the sides of the pot until they are fully extended, then trim these back by about a third. The tree is then returned to a smaller pot, probably no larger than 2 inches across and $1\frac{1}{2}$ inches deep, and fresh compost added. This must be packed in very tightly—the Japanese use a chopstick—so that the maximum soil is available.

Tiny stoneware pots for bonsai have large holes for drainage.

Leaf pruning is something that goes on throughout the growing season and consists of trimming selected leaves in half across the leaf. This encourages the development of other, smaller leaves, after which the original half-leaves drop off. Leaves should never be trimmed off as far back as the stalk; snip cleanly half-way down. Deciding which leaves to prune and which branches to stop is what bonsai is all about. An expert will take no less time than a beginner, and probably more, because the tree must be examined from all angles and its natural habit of growth encouraged and enhanced. Sometimes a specialist will do pruning, especially

root pruning, for you if you take your trees back to him; watching him work is an education in itself.

Properly grown, bonsai trees should be in the tiny frost-proof stoneware pots designed for them and usually imported from Japan. These have large holes in the base, so as to allow good drainage. Bonsai trees need regular watering but water must be able to drain away very freely.

For window ledge work you have two choices. You can dispense with the box and grow specimens in the correct Japanese pots, standing on the sill. Safer perhaps is to keep the tiny stoneware pots standing on gravel just inside a box so that they are contained within the box and less likely to be swept away by high winds or the incautious opening of a window. Essential, if you want to retain the sympathy of a specialist grower, is to grow them in the right pots; you really cannot expect him to take an interest in pruning your trees if you aren't growing them, according to his rules, properly.

You can also grow your own seedlings, or dig them up from your own or a friend's garden. Taking growing plants from the wild is now illegal and so it is irresponsible to suggest that you look for suitable specimens on the local common, although I cannot see you being marched off to prison if you should

carefully lift one tiny 4 inch birch seedling from among thousands in the wild. Wherever you find your seedling be sure to remove it very carefully, bringing as much soil as you can and not damaging the roots. Keep it in a sealed plastic bag until you are able to plant it in as small a pot as will comfortably take it. Don't at this stage prune the roots, other than trimming any that may have been damaged, but leave it to settle in for a few weeks. Once you see signs of new top growth you can begin leaf pruning, reducing top growth and encouraging the development of side growth. Never strip a tree of all its leaves, for these are essential to the process of photosynthesis by which plants live.

Seedlings, and indeed all bonsai specimens, should be planted in soil-based rather than soilless compost, sharpened further by the addition of horticultural grit or sand. Specialists often sell their own special mixes or you can concoct your own of JI 2, grit and so on. They may also sell special food, their own alternatives to the complicated diet of rice and soya beans that many Japanese growers devise. Or you can use houseplant food, diluted correctly and applied every ten days or so from May to September. Never feed a dry plant. Water it well first, then feed. And remember that as these trees

are denied the opportunity to put out large searching roots you must water them very often. In hot weather this may have to be morning, midday and evening, making sure that the water does not stand on leaves that are in full sun. A west-facing window ledge is ideal for growing bonsai as this means they have the advantage of good light but not the scorching midday sun.

Once you start taking an interest in bonsai you will probably notice trees grown all together in special plantings rather than in individual pots. These groupings, taken very seriously by the experts, are ideal for adapting to window box display. The aim is to produce a miniature landscape, and correctly this should be perfectly proportioned whichever way you look at it. For a window box that will be seen from the room only you can afford to be less exacting and build up a one-directional scene.

Soil, rocks, seedling trees or small cuttings, plus moss, are the usual ingredients of these landscapes, which are known as saikei, or bonkei if they contain a few artificial ornaments such as a tiny house, bridge, looking glass or real water lake and so on. Needless to say, a certain austerity is required when adding these if the whole thing is not to look like an overdecorated Christmas cake.

Fill the box with a much deeper than usual layer of gravel, then a top layer, 2 inches deep, of well-drained soil. Arrange rocks in a sweeping semi-circle, burying them well into the soil and making sure that the striations—the stripes that show up very clearly in some types of rock—line up in a natural way. Pile up the soil to make little foothills below the mountains, firming it well. Even more than when planning a mini-alp for an alpine box, the more time you spend at this stage the better. When you are happy with the contours, and have watered them well and left them for a few days to settle down, you can begin to plant seedling trees. Arrange them so that they all lean the same way, towards the rocks rather than away from them,

A careful grouping of seedling trees, well-marked rock and tasteful ornaments makes a Japanese-style miniature garden which is delightful for both adults and children. An arrangement can be fashioned in a conventional box, or in a shallow dish, and it is minute attention to proportion and detail which achieves the most exquisite effect.

Arrange seedling trees so that they lean towards nearby rocks.

Japanese maple
Acer palmatum

as wind most often blows towards mountains. You can have a tiny copse with a number, always an odd number, of trees, or just two or three. Arrange them to create a triangular outline, not an equilateral triangle but one with one steep side and one long sloping one. Stand back from time to time to gauge the effect, noting especially how it will look from a vantage point inside the room. Balance the picture with a single tree, add a winding path of fine gravel and mould the contours of the earth with different types of moss. This you may have to gather from the wild. It will not establish easily in its new home unless it is covered with more fine soil and sprayed with water regularly for a few days. At first the effect will not be very nice, just more mounds of earth, but after a week or so you should see signs of new growth. An alternative, if you have only a little moss, is to let it dry out thoroughly, break it down to a fine powder and sow it over your bare earth. Again, if it is regularly and gently watered with a fine spray, you should see new growth appearing in a week or two.

THE SCENTED BOX

There is something very evocative about scents drifting into the house from the garden on a warm summer evening. Philadelphus, the mock orange, usually still called syringa, and lilac, which really is syringa, are two of the most potent scented plants that you could contain in a large tub and station near a door or window. But it would take a few years for a young plant to reach a size sufficient to support a quantity of flowers and so the best subjects for a scented window box are likely to come from the long list of annual plants. These grow fast and will flower their heads off if conditions are right.

For summer evening scent there is really nothing to beat the tobacco plant, nicotiana. Of these the white are still the most fragrant, although scent is now coming back into the coloured forms too. If you have room, choose the old-fashioned white *Nicotiana alata*, which reaches 3 feet but is very strongly scented at night. Otherwise, go for the 16 inch Dwarf White Bedder, whose white scented

Concentrate perfume by planting nicotiana beside a window which you can open in the evenings.

flowers stay open all day. For colour as well as a certain amount of scent, 'Nicki' is only 12 inches tall and comes in pinks, white and lime green.

Stocks (matthiola) are another gloriously scented flower and the common or garden ten week stocks sold as bedding annuals are still among the most fragrant. They usually reach 18 inches, but there are now dwarf varieties which stop at 12 inches.

Alyssum (lobularia) has a sweet honey fragrance and now comes not only in basic white but in rose pink, as 'Rosie O'Day', and in deep purple, as 'Oriental Night'. The coloured ones are only slightly less fragrant than the white and all qualify for a place at the front of the box, as a tight-packed 3–4 inch border.

Dianthus, the original species from which the huge and largely unscented florists' carnations have been bred, are themselves richly scented. To be sure of scent, avoid the showy bicoloured and brightly coloured ones, often red, and select from those described as pinks. Because pinks here refers not to the colour, which can be anything from pure white to deepest red, but to the frilled, pinked edges of the leaves you can see that this is a very confusing species. The name to look out for is allwoodii, for these are the perpetual flowering, strongly scented

ones. Allwoodii 'Alpinus' comes in pink and lilac as well as white and is sweetly scented; it ranges in size from 6 to 12 inches, and if planted at the edge of a container will trail well. Really pendulous carnations are a familiar feature of window boxes in Switzerland and are now offered by a number of seed merchants. Look for names like *Caryophyllus* 'Luminette' if you like the idea, but for scent *C.* 'Crimson Knight' is hard to beat.

Lavender is another evocative old English scent and makes a good container plant, particularly if it can be tucked away out of sight once its flowering season is over and it has to be trimmed back hard. Later in the summer, when the new growth has appeared, the plants can be put on show again, for the grey domed bushes are still quite appealing. If lavender is not trimmed after flowering it soon becomes woody; it is a short-lived plant in any case and cuttings should be taken in August, from plants known to be well scented, using non-flowering shoots 3–4 inches long. Put half a dozen around the edge of a 5 inch pot of sandy compost and at least two or three, maybe all of them, will take and can be planted in the spring.

Rosemary is an invaluable plant for boxes and containers and is discussed elsewhere. Nevertheless,

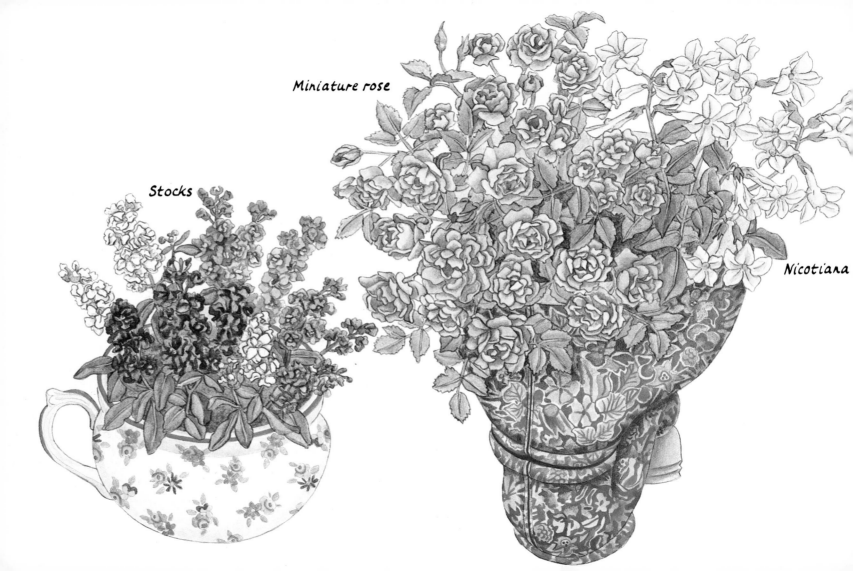

Miniature rose

Stocks

Nicotiana

it must be mentioned here for its place in a scented box. Thyme, too, has its value as a scented plant and just one in a scented box will also provide the occasional twig for the kitchen. Still among the herbs, there is southernwood, *Artemisia abrotanum*. This dies back in winter to a gnarled old stick, so it should go in a container that can be put out of sight for the season. *Anthemis nobilis* is the chamomile, which with enormous difficulty can be cultivated as a lawn. In a more easily weeded spot like a window box it will do better, particularly in full sun. The July flowers are white and daisy-like and there is a still better double form that I think is even more sweetly fruit-scented.

Back among the annuals again, you might try mignonette; reseda 'Red Monarch' has lovely fragrant red and green flowers up to 12 inches tall, but the taller 'Alba' (24 inches) has the true old-fashioned mignonette scent.

For spring scents there are the wallflowers, which you can plant after the summer annuals are over and that will give you a brave show of colour as well as scent. For best effect buy a single colour rather than a mixture and avoid anything that claims to offer the range of colours of an old Persian carpet. In a large bed in the open garden this is to my mind

only marginally effective; in a window box it looks untidy. 'Harpur Crewe' is a very old double-flowered wallflower with yellow flowers forming rounded spires and its scent is heady. The spires of erysimum look very much like wallflowers and appear at the same time but the plants are more compact and the leaves grey. The scent is not as strong as that of a wallflower but it is still a good fragrance. 'Bowles Purple' is tallish, at 2 feet; 'Moonlight' is yellow and has attractive chocolate brown buds but I wouldn't grow it for scent. Hyacinths are an obvious choice for spring scent but whether this has a chance to pervade the house depends largely on the weather and whether it is even remotely gentle enough to allow you to open a window.

Lily-of-the-valley (convallaria) is another headily scented plant. Not particularly attractive, unless removed from its broad surrounding leaves, but worth growing in a shady spot simply to provide a bunch to cut for indoor enjoyment.

Scented boxes can be colourful, and attractive too, if plants are massed in single-subject plantings. This is the way to concentrate the perfume, by planting just one subject and resisting the temptation to mix your plants. Mix up your scents and you lose the impact.

Sweetly-scented stocks come in shades of pink, crimson, lavender, white and yellow. Site them, in a pretty and unusual container, on a window sill or beside the door so you can enjoy their fragrance as you come and go. Roses, especially the old ones with their densely packed petals, are another scented pleasure while nicotiana is at its most headily fragrant at night.

THE HEATHER BOX

In the open garden, heaths and heathers must be tightly massed and viewed from something of a distance so that their softly coloured flowers and vivid foliage create a moorland vista in miniature.

In the window box or in any container that offers a close-up view, heathers take on a quite different but nonetheless attractive appearance. The flowers are small and bell-shaped, in pinks and purple and white, while the foliage, which can vary according to the time of year, ranges from yellow to green to bronze to grey.

Shopping for these plants in the garden centre, it is easy to be confused by the many names and labels. Strictly speaking, heaths are erica and heathers are *Calluna vulgaris,* of which *E. carnea* and *E. cinerea* are the most available low-growing varieties suitable for box work. Often also displayed in the heather or erica section are daboecia and phyllodoce. The most commonly found, *D. cantabrica*, can reach up to 3 feet in both height and spread, and as its flowers do not stay on the plant to provide winter interest it is perhaps not the best choice for a window box. Phyllodoce are generally smaller and more suitable for sinks and rock gardens.

This reduces the choice to two, ericas and callunas, from which you should choose according to size and time of flowering. You may also see a distinction made between those that hate lime and those that are lime-tolerant, but this is one you can ignore since you can make sure that the box is filled with a good peaty, and therefore lime-free, compost. Heathers need plenty of sun and should be planted well down so that the whole stem is buried and the foliage springs straight out of the compost. Once the woody stem protrudes the whole plant begins to look shabby, so keep it covered with an occasional mulch of peat. Heathers love peat but cannot, of course, be expected to thrive in pure peat; most garden centres sell an ericaceous mixture compost and this is ideal for an all-heather box. If you are combining heathers with other shrubs, add a little peat to the planting hole, plus a mulch around the plant. Of the many names you will see in a well-stocked heather section, *E. carnea* 'King George' has rose pink flowers, 'Winter Beauty' is another pink, 'Praecox Rubra' is deeper pink and

Heathers are good value plants. New growth is fresh and green, flowers are long lasting and foliage frequently colours well in autumn and winter. In close-up the flowers are surprisingly dainty, and the plants lend themselves well to display in unusual containers.

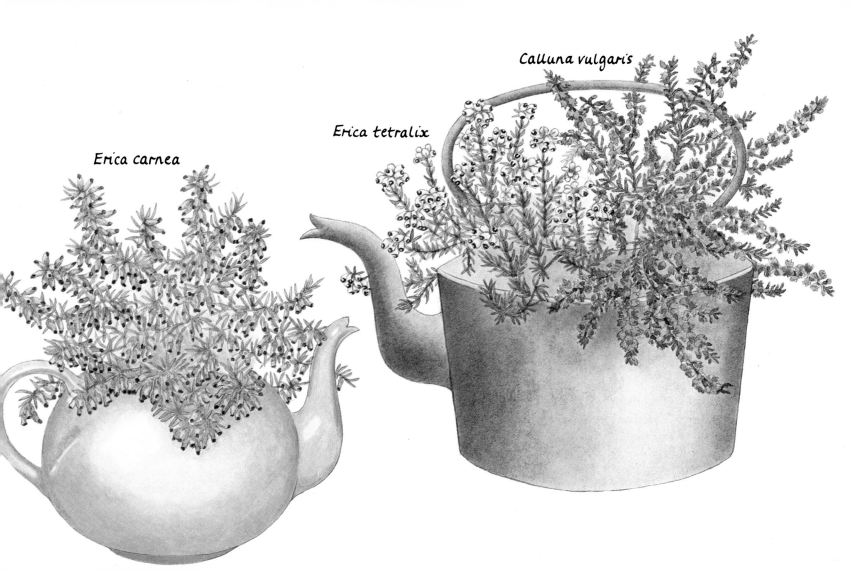

Erica carnea

Erica tetralix

Calluna vulgaris

'Loughrigg' combines pink buds opening to purple with green leaves that later turn bronze. These, with 'Springwood Pink' and 'Springwood White', will all provide winter flowers.

E. cinerea provides flowers between June and October and, as many of these fade to a russet brown after flowering, they are good value for most of the year. Varieties include 'Alba Minor' with white flowers and 'Atrorubens' with long-lasting red flowers; 'Cevennes' has pale lavender flowers and 'Velvet Night' flowers of a deep purple. Watch for height when choosing heathers. If you stick to varieties which go from 9 to 12 inches, and if you keep them trimmed, you should not be bothered by excess height and many will trail attractively over the edge of your box. But remember that some can reach 8 or 10 feet in height; E. arborea and E. lusitanica are definitely not for the window box.

THE BOX BOX

In a window box setting it might seem almost laughable to suggest topiary. But box, Buxus sempervirens, or Lonicera nitida — an unlikely member of the honeysuckle family— common thyme and rosemary can all be clipped to make hedges.

To make a hedge that can be crenellated like a castle keep, plant young bushes of box or Lonicera nitida—the dark green one, for best effect—packing the plants fairly close together in good compost. Trim them regularly; you can use kitchen scissors while the plant is young, keeping the top of the hedge level at first. Taper the hedge slightly, so that it is thicker at the base than at the top, and keep your top line level by using a length of string secured to stakes at either end as a guide. Once the hedge becomes established you can divide it up visually into sections, letting alternate ones grow up while preserving the original line. The shape should develop by letting growth go up and trimming it, rather than by biting down into the hedge to establish a lower level. Bit by bit the crenellations will establish, then all you will need to do is keep the whole thing trim.

Lonicera nitida grown as a garden hedge needs

cutting three or four times a year and should never be allowed to get away. Once it becomes scruffy through neglect it can never be redeemed by hard clipping but should be uprooted and started again. Fortunately it is easy to propagate from 4–6 inch cuttings popped into sandy compost. In a window box I would trim it every three or four weeks in the growing season.

Box is slower growing and so less likely to get out of hand. It makes a nice dense hedge if it is in good compost and regularly fed with something like Growmore. Yew, the traditional topiary plant, is even slower growing and is therefore less suitable for window box or container work. Rosemary is good, if you don't want to fashion it into anything too elaborate.

To achieve the traditional topiary shapes you build up a framework of wire and tie shoots into it. Wire of about the thickness of a cleaner's coathanger is about right, one end secured to the ground or side of the container. As the shoots grow, keep them tightly trimmed. Shaping should be done very gradually, as cutting too deeply into the growing bush could leave you with holes or bare patches. Since these and the necessary wire frame are not very decorative, it is perhaps best to have the more elaborate shapes in tubs that can be kept out of sight until they look more like a peacock and less like a mistake.

Since topiary takes time your hedging plants will have to stay in the same container for years and will quickly exhaust the compost. For this reason it is probably best to use soil-based rather than soilless compost. Scrape off the top couple of inches of soil in spring and replace it with fresh, using sterilized JI 3 and not garden soil, of course. In autumn a light dressing of bonemeal will help. Weeds, which are the bane of every newly established hedge in the open garden, are less of a problem in a window box but should nevertheless be removed whenever they do show. Light forking over of the soil at the same time will also keep moss at bay.

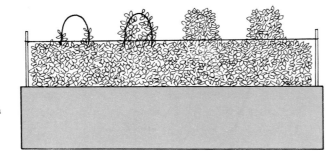

Use pegs and string to create a straight line to follow for clipping a tiny box hedge and wire for training.

A Box for the Cook

THE HERB BOX

Although it is doubtful whether many of the herbs so devotedly grown by herb gardeners are ever used there is no doubt that cooking would be a dull thing without the classic *bouquet garni* herbs. These and many others are easily raised in a fairly sunny window box and have the edge for immediate accessibility over those grown in the garden. All I would suggest is that you curb your enthusiasm for exotica such as alecost—tall, untidy, invasive and of precious little culinary value—or angelica—a six-footer whose stems can only with difficulty be candied—and use window box space to produce more useful and usable herbs.

The *bouquet garni* herbs, parsley, marjoram, thyme and bay, make in themselves a pleasant grouping; I would add chives, as much for their mauve pompom flower heads as for their fresh oniony leaves. Parsley is a hardy biennial tending to

flower and run to seed the spring after sowing. I sow it every year to ensure a constant supply. It is not only decorative, in the box and on the plate, but also rich in vitamins and iron; it is pretty nearly tasteless when dried, so well worth having fresh and close at hand. Parsley seed is slow to germinate but can be prodded into action if you soak it in warm water for twenty-four hours before sowing some time in March.

The wet seeds are then more difficult to space out in their seed box—they must be sown shallowly—but if you find you have sown too thickly you should thin out unwanted seedlings as soon as you can get hold of them. Use eyebrow tweezers if your fingers feel like thumbs. You are not supposed to transplant parsley unless you want a death in the family and it is also said to grow only if the woman of the house wears the trousers. Since it is also

Everyone likes the idea of growing herbs, but if space is limited make sure you grow only the most useful ones: parsley, mint, chives, basil for tomato dishes, marjoram for pizzas, coriander for curries and dill for fish. Plant them in attractive containers, and you have a feast for the eye as well as for your cooking pot.

Chives

Spearmint

Coriander

Marjoram

Parsley

Dill

Basil

Creeping thyme

supposed to go to the devil and back before it germinates you can decide for yourself whether you believe these old wives' tales. Use the older outside leaves of each plant first and keep picking to stimulate fresh growth and prevent bolting. You could save yourself trouble by buying ready raised plants of parsley, but this could be expensive as six plants would be the quantity necessary for a good supply.

Marjoram is the herb that gives pizza its distinctive flavour and is also an ingredient of the *bouquet garni*. One plant or possibly two should keep you supplied unless you are a real pizza freak so it is probably less trouble to buy plants from a nursery.

Look for *Origanum marjorana*, oregano or knotted marjoram, which is a perennial usually treated as an annual; it has a deliciously aromatic scent. *O. aureum* is the golden marjoram and probably the most attractive of the marjorams with tiny fresh greeny-gold leaves. This stays quite low at 9 inches and has a good flavour, though not as good as *O. marjorana*.

Thyme comes in a number of different types, from the tiny creeping *Thymus serpyllum* of the rock garden to the taller common thyme or lemon thyme, which is less pungent. One plant, possibly

Marjoram is the herb for pizza, and this perennial will give you a year-round supply.

two, should keep the modest cook well supplied with sprigs for a *bouquet garni* or chopped leaves for stuffing veal or chicken. It is a perennial that will keep you supplied throughout the year; trim the tips of the plant rather than yanking off a whole stem as this will keep it bushy. When it finally becomes

104

woody replace it with a new plant, possibly from a 3 inch cutting tucked in beside the mother plant. If you plant several of these in spring at least one should take to provide your new plant.

A bay leaf is the other classic ingredient of the *bouquet garni*. Bay is not easy to raise from seed or from cuttings and even small trees are not cheap to buy. It is probably best not to grow a bay tree in with the other herbs, but to keep it separate and undisturbed in its own plot. If you buy a new packet of dried bay leaves when you buy your small tree this will ensure that you don't rob it of leaves for the pot too early in its young life. Later, when it is more established, it will provide a constant supply of leaves for casseroles, tomato dishes and rice puddings. Bay can be tender and even an established plant can be cut down by prolonged frost so it is as well to bring the pot into the kitchen during bitter weather.

Chives have a milder flavour than onion and a few leaves can be snipped over potatoes or potato salad or added to omelettes to enhance the flavour. Buy a small plant and grow it in a sunny box and it will soon increase in size. In winter it will die back and may perish altogether; if you divide the plant up at the end of summer and pot the small bits

individually you will increase your chances of having a survivor. Bring one pot into the kitchen at the beginning of spring to force it into growth for an early supply of leaves.

Sage you will need only infrequently unless you are mad about sage and onion stuffing. It makes an attractive plant, however, if you have the space. There is a purple-leaved variety that is colourful and well flavoured and you may also see a yellow and green one—*Salvia officinalis* 'Icterina'—or the variegated white, green and pink form known as 'Tricolor', but these are perhaps best grown for decoration rather than flavouring. Sage likes plenty of sun and should be picked over regularly to keep it bushy; replace it when it becomes too gnarled and woody, again from cuttings tucked in beside their mother in the spring.

Basil is one herb I cannot be without and as it is rarely available fresh in the shops it is well worth finding space for in the window box. If you want enough for pesto sauce you will have to devote an entire box or other container to it. Otherwise a couple of plants should supply leaves for snipping over tomato salads. Basil is an annual that grows easily from fairly large seeds that can be spaced out neatly in a small pot. Surplus plants can be grown

indoors to provide thoughtful gifts for a hostess or even extra supplies for yourself. Keep the plants bushy by removing the tips and don't on any account let basil flower—pick off buds as soon as you see them—or the plant will pack up and die, its life's work fulfilled.

Mint is an essential herb if you like it with new potatoes or as mint sauce with lamb. Yet I doubt the wisdom of planting it in a window box as it will take it over in no time. Grow it in a pot on its own, as large and deep as you have room for, and you will have the best of both worlds, a good supply of mint and no harm done to your other herbs. For culinary use buy the large woolly-leaved *Mentha rotundifolia* 'Bowles Variety'. Alternatively, leave a bunch of well-flavoured sprigs in water, changing this before it turns sour, and before long you will see them throwing out tiny white roots. Plant a few in good compost and you will soon have plants for picking. Mint suffers from rust in the garden, especially if it is in an old neglected colony. If you see the characteristic orange spores on your plants pull them up and get rid of them and the compost and start again with new clean plants.

In garden centres you will see an increasing number of different types of mint: eau de cologne with purplish leaves, pineapple with white edges, ginger, green striped with yellow, and other exotica. People fall on each new variety with cries of delight and home it goes to send its creeping runners throughout the garden, strangling every plant it meets. These strangely scented mints have little culinary worth but can be grown in individual containers for their novelty value and for their scent. Plant them in the open garden at your peril.

Rosemary can reach up to 6 feet in a warm spot in the garden but as it is not a fast-growing plant can easily be accommodated in the window box. One small plant should be enough to provide occasional snippings for roast lamb; it should be used judiciously as too much rosemary makes things bitter. It likes the sun and can be cut down by frost in winter, although it is often the older bushes which succumb while the young ones survive. Buy a small plant, pick off the tips rather than removing branches and bring it indoors in very bad weather. A fully grown bush of rosemary such as *R. officinalis* 'Miss Jessup's Upright' in an 8 or 10 inch pot beside the kitchen door makes attractive and useful decoration, pleasantly aromatic to brush past or rub between the fingers as you go by. The blue flowers appear in spring and then intermittently through the summer.

After the first flush of flowers trim the plant into a neat shape, reserving the trimmings for kitchen use.

These are the herbs I find useful and that I think warrant a place in the limited confines of a window box or other container. In any well-stocked nursery or garden centre you will be sure to find many others, often enthusiastically recommended for serving with broad beans, fish, rhubarb, or whatever. Whether you need these depends, I suppose, on your intake of broad beans, rhubarb, etc. If you are inordinately fond of broad beans you could grow summer savory, an annual that should be giving you shoots for cutting in June along with the first of the beans.

Herbs are something of a cult at the moment and it is all too easy to get carried away and end up giving tender loving care to a coarse unlovely weed. The same commodity, tlc, expended on good culinary herbs to go with your favourite dishes is another thing entirely.

THE VEGETABLE BOX

In the days when half an acre was regarded as a small garden the idea of growing vegetables in window boxes would have been a huge joke. Today, with our smaller plots and smaller families, the idea is not so laughable. Seedsmen, too, have been working for us to produce dwarfer, tidier plants that can be accommodated in boxes, tubs and other containers. There are, too, the ubiquitous growing bags so that anyone with a fancy for home-grown beans or peppers or tomatoes or other salad crops can easily indulge this. All right, you will hardly have surplus for freezing but you should be able to enjoy good early pickings. And what a triumph, to be able to serve French beans with a real snap to them, freshly picked from your own window sill. French beans, especially the dwarf varieties that need no staking, are a vegetable particularly suited to container growing. Sow a dozen seeds in a standard growing bag, which is usually 3 feet long and 18 inches wide. There are also mini bags suitable for small spaces and crops. Sometimes bags may be cheaper but slightly smaller than standard and may not be so great a bargain if they support fewer plants. So buy the largest you have room for. If you have no room for a growing bag but must plant in the window box, you should space out beans at 4–6 inches apart, thinning as they germinate to 8–12 inches apart. Look for a variety such as 'Cyrus', which produces those slim round crisp pods served in any modest restaurant in France but in only the grandest elsewhere. The beans should be planted 1 inch, or a little more, deep some time between mid-April and early May depending on the weather. The plants of 'Cyrus' reach 18 inches and the crop comes early. Start feeding with a proprietary feed as soon as you pick the first beans and this will encourage subsequent crops. Keep the compost moist at all times, but not wet.

Tomatoes are probably the most frequently grown growing bag crop and many gardeners with plenty of open ground still prefer this method of cultivation. For one thing it is easier to water a relatively small bag, and for another it can be sited close to a sunny wall to encourage earlier crops. Tomato plants can be raised from seed sown in mid-April in heat and pricked out and carefully tended indoors until early June when it is safe to plant outdoors. Seed will certainly give you the variety of your choice but now that garden centres are offering a wider range—from the big ugly 'Marmande' to the tiny cherry-sized 'Sweet 100'—it is infinitely easier to buy plants. Choose sturdy green ones with their first flowers just showing and avoid those that have a blue tinge—they have been chilled—or straggly yellow ones that are past their best. Plant three tomatoes per growing bag, or four if you have 'Sweet 100', which makes a taller, less bushy plant.

Some sort of support will be necessary, either one of the specially devised but admittedly rather expensive support systems for growing bags, or wires wrapped around the bag and secured to an adjacent wall or fence. Tomatoes can also be grown in 12 inch pots, where they can be provided with the more usual stake; do this at the same time as you transfer the plants from the pots in which they were bought so that you don't disturb the roots.

To encourage tall, fruit-bearing plants you must be diligent about removing the side shoots that develop in the leaf axils. Tie the plant to its support loosely but at regular intervals and pick out the tip when it has set four or five trusses. Encourage fruit to set by gently shaking the plants from time to time to scatter the pollen; you may have to do this more

often if your plants are high up on a balcony and bees and other insects have not yet discovered them. Tomatoes need plenty of water, and feeding as soon as the first truss has set. Use a proprietary tomato food rather than a general purpose one, and follow the instructions as to quantity and dilution. More is not better when it comes to feeding plants.

Peppers are not easy to crop in the open garden unless the summer is particularly benign but are often successful in boxes, bags or pots close to the house where they can benefit from the heat bounced off the walls. Buy plants from a nursery for planting and staking as soon as the first flower opens, usually around the same time as tomatoes, in early June. Feed with tomato fertilizer and water well. Treat them much as you do tomatoes in fact, although no side shooting is necessary. To keep fruit coming pick it regularly when green; if you leave it to turn red on the plant you will reduce the crop severely. Green peppers left in a warm dry place will turn red of their own accord in time.

Aubergines (eggplants) are worth a try if you like them or Greek moussaka of which they are an essential ingredient. Again they do best against a sunny wall, three to a standard growing bag, with support for the stems. Buy plants and set in position

as soon as the first flowers open, or they will grow away too fast and not get fruit. There is no need to remove side shoots, but taking out the growing tips when they reach 1 foot encourages bushy plants with two main shoots rather than one. In hot weather the flowers can be syringed occasionally to help fruit to form. Regular feeding with a tomato fertilizer will also be necessary as, of course, will regular watering. Vegetables are very largely composed of water so it is inevitable that they need a lot.

Cucumbers have come on a great deal since the old days when they needed expert attention to get anything other than a miserable crop of bitter fruit. There are now all-female varieties that save you the effort of removing the male flowers that produce bitter fruit and there are also bitter-free varieties. Nevertheless, cucumbers are something of a specialist crop. If you feel like trying them, buy ready-grown plants and put them three to a growing bag or singly in pots. The outdoor or ridge varieties are easiest and for a novelty crop you could try to get hold of plants of 'Crystal Apple', which, for some reason or other, produces cucumbers the size, shape and colour of a large lemon. 'Sweet Success' is an all-female plant that can be grown out of doors in

Aubergines (Eggplants)

French beans

Sweet peppers

Chili peppers

Bush tomato
(Cherry tomato)

a container and 'Patio-Pik' claims to take up no more room than a cabbage and endure neglect yet still produce more than thirty cucumbers per plant. I haven't tried it myself but, even allowing for a bit of horticultural hyperbole, it sounds just the thing for the window box gardener.

Salad crops, which must be grown fast to be really succulent, are good subjects for a window box. Sow lettuce seed—make sure it is new season's seed—ten or twelve to a bag in early April and keep the compost moist but not sopping wet. Thin out the young plants to six; with luck you will be able to have a small salad from even these thinnings. As the remaining lettuces develop keep them well watered by trickling water around the plants, trying not to splash the leaves. Cut the lettuce with a sharp knife when hearted but still young and juicy. The first crop in a growing bag will not need feeding but the second crop, which you can sow as soon as the first is done but not later than the end of July, will need regular feeding.

Radishes will grow well even in a small window box, sown in late March along a ½ inch deep drill. As the roots develop you thin them out and if lucky you can use the thinnings in salads. Regular watering is essential to ensure juicy radishes but, all things considered, I feel better use than this can be made of the summer window box or an expensive growing bag.

All kinds of squash, courgettes (zucchini), marrows and even pumpkins can be grown in containers and bags. Courgettes (zucchini) are the best bet, cut while small so as to encourage more fruit to form. Plant two to a standard bag and choose bush rather than trailing varieties as the latter can be terrible wanderers. Plants carry both male and female flowers, the latter being recognizable by the tiny swelling courgette just behind the flower. Usually the first flowers to appear are male and as soon as you can see a female you must remove a male, strip the petals off and push the pollen-covered spike into that female flower. Eventually more female flowers will develop and insects will do the job of pollination for you. Regular watering and picking is all that should be required to keep the plants going until the first frosts, although an occasional feed will also help.

Marrows are grown the same way but plants are restricted to only two or three fruit, which must be left to develop and will also need feeding. For a monster marrow to show off to your friends—don't think it will be edible—you can thread a length

Tyres (tires) make surprisingly large containers which are very suitable for growing vegetables. Plant tender subjects like peppers and aubergine (eggplant) and keep them in a sunny spot. Feed them regularly, and give them all the water they love and you will be rewarded with modest, but none-the-less, welcome crops.

of wool through a small hole made in the stem about an inch away from the fruit. Immerse the other end in a jar of sugar solution, one teaspoonful of sugar to a 1 pound jam jar; if you conceal this under leaves no-one will know that you are cheating.

Pumpkin can be grown the same way, one to a plant. The resulting fruit can be turned into pumpkin pie or cut and left in a corner of the kitchen in the hope that it will turn into a fairy coach. Mine hasn't, yet.

Other marrow varieties include delightful scallop-shaped fruit called 'Custard Yellow' or 'Patty Pan'. These taste exactly like courgettes (zucchini) but have the virtue of this novelty shape. In the open garden, where yield tends to be more important, some of these novelties may not be very successful. But in a confined space where yield will never be high it is worth growing them because they are so different from anything you can buy in the shops.

Seed raisers have been experimenting in the last year or two with vegetables that can be grown in hanging baskets. I have seen bush tomatoes, the ones that are not stopped or de-shooted but allowed to spread along the ground on straw, planted one to a basket and growing nicely. Yield, it has to be said, is

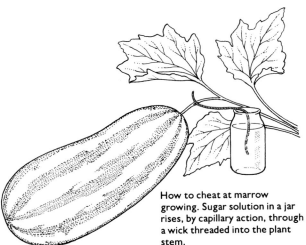

How to cheat at marrow growing. Sugar solution in a jar rises, by capillary action, through a wick threaded into the plant stem.

Start the bean in an upturned bottle, supported in a patch of spare ground, then invert the bottle and hang it. The beanstalk will then climb skywards.

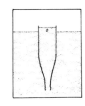

not heavy and towards the end of the summer the yellowing of the lower leaves, which is normal, makes for a less than decorative appearance. However, for novelty value, and for an occasional picking of sweet homegrown tomatoes, you could certainly try a few plants in baskets. Make sure you buy bush tomato plants—'Sigmabush' or 'Primabel' or, if you can find it, 'Minibel'—and keep them well watered and fed.

Something else that you could do for novelty value rather than for heavy cropping is to grow runner beans in wine bottles. The bottoms must first be tapped out of the bottles using a hammer and a cold chisel. This is not as difficult as it sounds. Up-end the bottles—I usually 'plant' them in a spare place in the garden pro tem—and fill tightly with good compost, tucking a couple of beans in, each an inch or so deep, as you go. Keep watered and when germination has taken place remove the bottles from wherever you have been supporting them and tie around their necks lengths of string that can be used to hang them from a convenient place. As the emerging shoots grow, thin to one per bottle. It will curl around the bottom of the bottle to grow upwards, as it ought. You can then encourage it around the sides of the bottle and up the strings from which it hangs. Watering and liquid feeding is done through the narrow top of the bottle and flowers and a few beans should be your reward. By no means the way to grow massive crops, but a novelty that might amuse the children.

THE FRUIT BOX

In the large estates of the past, with their lovely walled kitchen gardens, acres of glass and abundance of labour, fruit was often grown in pots. Even exotics like oranges and lemons were planted in large planters provided with wheels, so that when summer came the trees could be moved out of the orangery into a sunny position in the open. Pineapples and grapes were grown under glass, and great was the pressure on the poor gardeners to provide early fruit for the table.

Today few of us have the time or means for all this to-ing and fro-ing of pots and, besides, the shops are full of oranges and lemons, grapes and pineapples, usually throughout the year. You could have an orange or a lemon or a grapefruit tree in a pot on the patio and move it to a cool greenhouse or a conservatory during the winter, but even then the most you would be likely to see would be the occasional flower. Still, the plants will come, from pips (pits) sown in pots of moist compost kept close (see pp. 29–37) and with bottom heat if possible. In as little as three years you could have a 5 foot tree

with attractive dark green shiny leaves. But fruit, no.

Date stones too can be sown in a plastic bag of moist compost kept in the airing cupboard and inspected regularly. At the first signs of sprouting the stones must be removed and planted and kept close for a bit. Eventually a long, drab spike of a leaf appears, followed by other long, drab spikes. But dates, no.

Avocado stones can be set, sharp end upwards, half in and half out of water until either roots appear from below or the water becomes stagnant and smelly and the whole thing has to be thrown away. If roots do appear, and this happens fairly often, they can be left to develop for a few weeks then planted in compost, the stone still not quite covered. The final appearance will be fairly spectacular and a real tribute to your gardening skills on the patio in the summer and indoors in winter. But fruit, you've guessed it, no.

Apples will grow from seeds, not into the Cox or the Ellison of the parent but into sour little crabs more than likely. Nevertheless you could have blossom in a pot on the patio in spring and the satisfaction of having raised a plant from a seed. Grapes, too, will come from seeds, and yet again these will not be luscious Black Hamburgs but grapes

that can only be described as sour. You will have a vine, though, and vine leaves for making dolmades.

All sorts of fruit stones and pips (pits) can be tried and many will provide unusual greenery, to be regarded as decoration only. And if all this seems too much of a turn-off let me, before you throw the book down in disgust, move on to figs and strawberries. These are two fruits that are worth growing for their fruit, in pots, containers or, in the case of strawberries, in a box.

Figs, even when raised in the open or in a greenhouse, are best grown with their roots restricted. Outdoors this very often means digging a deep cement-lined pit, but a 12 inch pot could be just as effective in restricting root growth and preventing the development of over-lush top growth. Figs need the protection of a sunny wall or a corner between south and west walls and even then the pot will probably need to be wrapped in sacking and straw during the winter. In hard winters the whole tree may need to be protected by a curtain of sacking or heavy net, opened up to let the air in during milder spells. Quite a lot of bother but worth doing, especially if you are besotted about fresh figs, which many people are.

Even more of us are besotted about strawberries

Strawberries adapt well to life in a barrel and should crop for three years before needing replacement. Watch out for slugs as the fruit ripens. Birds are best discouraged by keeping a mean cat.

and here the process is a good deal simpler. Barrels provided with planting holes, or terracotta planting pots with similarly distributed holes, make a most attractive sight when filled with merrily flowering and then ripening fruit. The plastic planters sold for the purpose are less pleasing to look at in themselves but equally good for growing good clean fruit, while growing bags and boxes can be used for alpine strawberries. These are rather more of a myth than a meal, since they tend to produce too little fruit at one time to satisfy anything but the most elfin appetite. But they are undeniably a treat.

Strawberries today can be had as traditional June croppers or as a late summer crop. Whichever you decide upon be sure to buy good clean plants, certified as virus-free. There is no profit in cultivating diseased plants and this may include rooted runners given you by a kindly friend, so be warned. Plants should go into a good soil compost, John Innes 3 for instance, although the peat-based compost found in growing bags is equally good. The plants go in during July or early August, are overwintered in a sheltered spot and brought into a sunny place in spring when growth begins again. Fruit can usually be taken the first year, provided that the plants are put in by July. After a later

planting it is usually advisable to pick off flowers and wait a year for a fruit crop, but for container-grown plants this seems a bit pointless. So get your plants in early and take a crop the first year.

If planting in a barrel, insert plants as you go up the barrel, firming them in carefully and adding the next layer of soil. Before you get too far, insert a roll of chicken wire or a length of garden hose punctured every inch or so to act as a drainage pipe. If this stands on the initial layer of drainage material that must go at the bottom of every deep planter, it will allow water to spread outwards through the entire pot as well as downwards from the top. The top layer of a barrel or strawberry pot could take perhaps five or six plants spread out around the rim so that they will hang down the pot. This saves applying the traditional layer of straw or less traditional black polythene that protects the fruit from splashes and slugs. Trailing sweetly down the sides of the planter they won't need this protection, but don't think they will be safe from the birds. The best you can do about these little dears is to cover the whole thing with net; you may spoil the decorative appearance but at least save the fruit. Or get a mean and hungry cat.

Grown in a barrel your plants should give you a

Dwarf apple tree in a classic container—an attractive idea but don't expect a heavy crop.

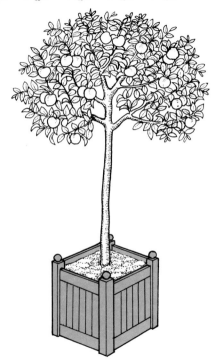

each year into a fresh bag. You can use the old bag again, for a quick crop of lettuce in spring. Or plant the strawberries in July in a bag that has just produced some early lettuces. Don't apply feed at planting time but in the following spring as growth starts.

Having been somewhat dismissive of fruit in pots, I have to admit that a great deal of work is being done by growers to produce dwarf trees. Apples, even in the open orchard, are now grown on much shorter trees to make picking easier, and some of these dwarf trees are being offered for sale, ready planted in large tubs, by adventurous garden centres. They are not cheap to buy but if the fancy takes you you could have a Cox's Orange Pippin, or even a family tree that carries more than one type of apple, on your sunny patio or balcony. Make sure you get explicit advice on how to care for the tree and, more particularly, how to prune it. If such advice is not forthcoming you might be advised to resist the temptation to buy. Some trees are self-fertile, others need another nearby for pollination and subsequent fruiting. In short, the whole subject of growing top fruit is complex and the wrong tree, wrongly cared for and in the wrong place, could be an expensive disappointment.

crop for three years as long as you feed them after cropping and stop the formation of runners. After that throw them away and begin again with fresh stock. You could also leave strawberries in a growing bag for three years but I prefer to replant

A Box for the Children

THE GNOME GARDEN BOX

It is fashionable to reel in horror at the thought of gnomes in the garden but it has to be said that children usually love them. They also fall for cement ducks and frogs, for plastic toadstools and windmills and wells, complete with bucket and chain. Disparity of size or materials doesn't seem to bother children either, so a window sill garden of small shrubs and large gnomes or large shrubs and small gnomes would probably delight its young owner.

It goes without saying that only children who can be trusted to lean out of the window or who are carefully supervised should be allowed a gnome garden box. Your local garden centre will probably reveal a rich source of possible subjects. As with all collections, it is best to have a theme so if the first choice is a jolly gnome with a fishing rod you should give him something to fish in. An old china dish might do, or even a plastic fridge container, as long

Gnomes may not be everyone's cup of tea, but children usually adore them. They can add a touch of whimsy to a group of individually potted shrubs or can feature in a box of their own, complete with mini pond and even fish.

Hide the edges of the mini-pool with carefully arranged pebbles in your children's gnome box.

118

Hibiscus rosa-sinensis

Potentilla fruticosa

Hydrangea macrophylla

as the edges can be concealed with small stones or rocks. The bottom could be decorated with gravel, which will support a few marginal plants from the water section in the garden centre or even from a local supplier of tropical fish. These can be rooted in the gravel and, barring accidents, should last a season before succumbing to frost, although some cold-water plants will survive.

Hornwort (ceratophyllum) is one. It has fine light green leaves set on a long waving stalk rather like the needles on a branch of pine. Elodea makes rosettes that grow above the water and is also pretty tough. These cold-water plants are inexpensive; they are usually sold in bunches held together with a lead strip to weight them down. You plant them still in their bunches and if they like their new quarters they will quickly expand.

Another possibility is the indoor plant *Cyperus alternifolius*, the umbrella plant. This has thin stems topped by umbrellas of thin leaves and it does best if its roots are always wet. Settled into place still in its pot in a few inches of water it will probably romp away, as long as it is not in strong sunlight. You will have to bring it indoors again for the winter, though.

Your gnome garden pond might even contain a couple of tiny fish, a pair of golden medakas that will survive cold but not frost; they could be brought indoors for the coldest months. To support fish you need at least the smallest size of cold-water aquarium. Seek advice from a local petshop so that there is no possibility of cruelty to the fishy denizens of your gnome garden pond window box. Alongside the pond you could grow primulas and polyanthus that like a moist atmosphere, mimulus, particularly the low-growing rock garden ones like *M. luteus* 'Alpinus', or *Lysimachia nummularia*, which is a vigorous trailing waterside plant with yellow buttercup flowers, better known perhaps as creeping jenny.

Less aquatic gnomes, ones that sit cross-legged on a toadstool for instance, could live in a forest garden made up of miniature conifers such as have been suggested for the alpine box. A handful of the finest grass seed can be sown to make a little glade between the trees.

If a Siamese cat fashioned in concrete is the chosen occupant of your children's box then it would only be sensible to surround him with catmint, *Nepeta faassenii*, with narrow grey-green leaves and spikes of lavender flowers in summer. *N. hederacea* is lower growing and neater and *N.h.* 'Variegata' has white marked leaves and is often

chosen for less whimsical window boxes. Another touch of whimsy might be a tortoise—plastic or cement, of course—in a bed of lettuce, or Peter Rabbit himself in a box of carrots.

A more practical suggestion for older, conservation-minded children might be to cultivate some of our vanishing wild flowers in a window box, letting them set seed in the hope that this will be carried off in the wind to find a home somewhere. This is not too fanciful a suggestion, either. The Oxford ragwort, now fairly common in waste patches in the south of England, is an escapee from the Oxford Botanic Garden and the downy seed is said to have first travelled down railway lines in the slipstream of trains.

More recently, oil seed rape, planted by British farmers for its subsidy as much as anything and which makes those searing stretches of yellow in May, is now appearing along the roadside and is currently making its way towards central London via Hackney Marshes. Some seedsmen now specialize in wild flower seed, either in mixtures suitable for certain types of soil or in single species packets. For a sandy soil, for instance, they offer a mix containing lady's bedstraw, birdsfoot trefoil, buttercup, meadow campion, foxglove, harebell, wild mignonette, yellow rattle, lesser vetch, viper's bugloss and yarrow. The seeds come in a mix with the appropriate grass seeds, the idea being to create a mini-meadow. Quite small quantities can be ordered, which makes it an option for a window box or container.

Finding out the names of plants once common and now less so, or vanished from their own locality, could be a holiday project for older children, to be followed up by a purchase of seeds and their cultivation. Even in cities that are rapidly becoming concreted over, these might eventually find a home and establish. While growing in a window box, of course, they can be examined close up, and enjoyed for their tiny delicate blooms.

THE PIP (PIT) BOX

The range of exotic fruit available from supermarkets is increasing all the time. Sometimes the expensive purchase turns out to be a bit of a disappointment, possibly because in our ignorance it is eaten before it is ripe or because, like the fig, it is really only nice when eaten straight off the tree.

Planting the stones, however, can be very rewarding. Children, and adults too for that matter, can plant orange, lemon and grapefruit seeds in pots of moist compost. Lemons are easiest to raise, and then grapefruit, but I have had least success with oranges. All will make shapely shrubs that can be grown in window box or tub; they may even bear sweetly scented white flowers but are highly unlikely to bear fruit. Pomegranate makes first a shrub and then a tree with tiny reddish leaves and in a very hot summer it might even produce flowers, though not fruit. My four year old pomegranate is now in a 10 inch pot and spends the winter in a heated greenhouse because it is both delicate and partly deciduous; if I had no greenhouse I would overwinter it indoors, where it would drop all its leaves but still survive. Kiwi fruit contains hundreds of tiny black seeds that germinate well if spread out on top of, rather than under, soilless compost. They will eventually grow, with the minimum of fuss, into attractive climbers with rather hairy reddish leaves. They need some support and if you take out the tops you will encourage side shoots. Passion fruit have quite large seeds; the plant has large leaves cut like a fig leaf when mature, and attractive curling tendrils. The flowers of this *Passiflora edulis* are not quite as showy as those of the more commonly grown *P. caerulea* and the chances of fruit are not high, but it is nevertheless a super plant to have produced in this way. Peanuts taken from carefully crushed shells can make quite an attractive show in a window box. The leaves are clover-like and the flowers like tiny yellow sweet peas. A bonus for children is that the plant can often be persuaded, if it has enough room, to produce a further supply of underground nuts.

Grape seeds germinate readily into tiny vines but it must be said that these rarely produce luscious fruit, despite what you may hear to the contrary. However, a grape vine from a seed planted in a tub

Avocado pits and orange and lemon pits will all make attractive green-leaved bushes. You may have a few failures at first with avocado, but success will bring a well-shaped plant with large glossy leaves. Lemon, grapefruit and orange pits start into growth more readily and again produce well-shaped bushes. Flowers and fruit could follow, once the bushes are well established in good sized pots.

Avocado

Peach

Grapefruit

Orange

at ground level can be trained up trellis and will eventually produce flowers and fruit of sorts. Before this, of course, it is a source of colour, particularly in autumn when the leaves turn, and also a source of leaves for dolmades and other Greek dishes.

Date pits should be chitted to encourage germination and this means soaking them in warm water forty-eight hours, then popping them into damp peat in a polythene bag and leaving this in the airing cupboard or somewhere equally warm. Inspect the bag every week and water the peat if it seems at all dry, extracting any stones that are starting to show roots. Pot these and keep them moist and warm, but in the light. Eventually a few spikes of sharp leaves will appear, and although these are not very exciting to look at a child might be thrilled with his own homegrown date palm. A better subject for a pot than for a window box, as it will have to be brought indoors for the winter.

Avocados can make 60 foot trees in the wild so these too are better for a pot than a box. The snag is getting the pits to germinate, as many seem to fail for no good reason. I find it best to soak them for forty-eight hours in warm water in the airing cupboard then stand them, round side down, on one of those glasses sold for growing hyacinth bulbs in

water rather than in soil. The idea is to keep the root end always just into some warm water, and if you are in luck the first roots will appear within three weeks or so. You can let these develop into a well-branched mass before transferring them into compost in a pot, as the pit itself contains plenty of nourishment. The rooting pit should be buried half in and half out of the compost, then a shoot will appear and develop a topknot of leaves. Now comes the hard bit. When this is 6 inches high you must snip off the topknot and 2 inches of shoot; this encourages the plant to make a bush rather than a single-stemmed tree. The 4 inch leafless twig looks a bit sad at first but will soon break again with new shoots and tufts of leaves. From then on you will have to prune the plant occasionally to encourage further bushy growth and leaf, rather than stem, production. Avocados like a fair amount of water and plenty of light and the leaves should be sprayed or sponged to keep them glossy. With luck and a following wind, the plant will have been repotted until it is in its final 10 or 12 inch pot within a few years. No likelihood of fruit in our temperate climate unfortunately, but the plant itself is very presentable as a patio subject.

Less exotic homegrown fruit will also come from

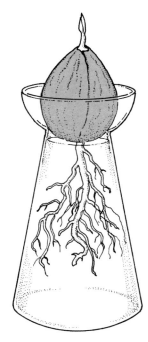

Use a hyacinth glass to hold the avocado pit just clear of the water. The rooting system will be vigorous.

pips (pits). Apples are not very likely to produce good fruit and tend to go back to the original crab apple. Peaches on the other hand do come true and stories about richly fruiting trees that came from stones are often genuine. Apple seeds should be planted when ripe, that is usually black or dark brown, and germinate fairly easily. Peaches and other stone fruit take longer, and attempts to get them to germinate in pots often fail because enthusiasm for watering wanes long before the poor thing has a chance to show signs of top growth. Children, particularly, like to see results quickly, so it is perhaps unrealistic to expect them to take an interest in stone fruit. One gardener I know buries an assortment of stones in spare soil in a greenhouse that is always kept well watered for other crops. Those stones that do germinate he plants in pots and gives away as presents, having long since filled his own sunny, sheltered garden positions.

As discussed before, fruit grown in pots is unlikely to produce a worthwhile crop. But to raise young plants for your own or someone else's garden, a container or other planter pot is ideal.

THE SPECIAL COLOUR BOX

When a local football team is heading for success enthusiastic fans have been known to show their support by plantings in the team colours. As these are usually good primary colours, like red or blue with white, this is quite easy to do.

Silver plants that could celebrate a family silver wedding are often found in the herb garden. *Cineraria maritima*, which has recently become *Senecio bicolor*, is perhaps the best known and is widely used for window boxes as it is pretty tough. To preserve the all-silver look, cut off the yellow daisy flowers as they appear; they are not in any case very attractive. *Senecio laxifolius*, usually confused with *S. greyi*, and *vice versa*, is another silver subject with yellow flowers that are best removed.

Artemisias are also grown for their silver, aromatic foliage rather than for their insignificant yellow flower heads. *A. absinthium* in its good silver form 'Lambrook Silver' can get to 3 feet. *Helichrysum angustifolium*, the curry plant, is lower at 10–15 inches, and has silver needle-like leaves that give off a distinct curry smell. *H. splendidum*, which can get to 3 feet if allowed but which can be clipped hard in spring to keep it down to 15 inches or so, has downy silver foliage. Some nurseries specialize in silver plants and if you can get to one you will probably find plants that are correctly labelled and will therefore perform as expected. In garden centres and among gardeners themselves there is often confusion and downright incorrect labelling, and this can be a problem if you are buying for a small window box.

Blue and white is a mixture that is easy enough to organize. Lobelia and alyssum spring immediately to mind and in a large enough box you might—should you have a mind—be able to spell out CHELSEA in alyssum against the blue of lobelia. For a patriotic British box you could include some of the new red lobelia for a red, white and blue effect. If you carry patriotism to extremes and wish to proclaim your allegiance to Scotland, you could fashion the cross of St Andrew in blue and white. However, Americans, even Texans with their obviously larger window boxes, would have trouble getting in all the stars and stripes, although they might try.

Children love the wide-awake blooms of the lily-flowered and kaufmanniana tulips. They make strong blocks of colour and can be planted to make bold striking patterns—perhaps incorporating the colours of your favourite football team. For more detailed effect—to pick out a name or outline a flag—choose smaller plants. Alyssum and lobelia are frequently used this way.

Darwin hybrid
'Jewel of Spring'

Lily-flowered tulip
'China Pink'

Tulipa kaufmanniana
'Shakespeare'